HESI A2 MATH PRACTICE TESTS

HESI A2 Nursing Entrance Exam Math Study Guide

The HESI Admission Assessment is a trademark of Elsevier Inc, which is not affiliated with nor endorses this publication.

© COPYRIGHT 2018
Exam SAM Study Aids & Media dba www.examsam.com

All rights reserved. No part of this publication may be reproduced, stored in a retrieval system, or transmitted, in any form or by any means, electronic, mechanical, photocopying, recording, or otherwise.

ISBN 13: 978-0-9998087-2-6
ISBN 10: 0-9998087-2-6

COPYRIGHT NOTICE TO EDUCATORS: Please respect copyright law. Under no circumstances may you make copies of these materials for distribution to students. Should you wish to use the materials in a classroom, you need to purchase a copy for each of your students in order to comply with copyright law.

For information regarding bulk discounts please contact us at: email@examsam.com

The HESI Admission Assessment is a trademark of Elsevier Inc, which is not affiliated with nor endorses this publication.

How to Use this Publication

You should study the tips and example problems in HESI practice test 1 with the math concept and formula review first.

Practice test 1 is in study guide format, providing the answers and explanations directly below each question.

The solution is with the question so that you can see more clearly how to solve the problem and study all of the steps in the solution.

You may wish to work through practice test 1 with a piece of paper to cover up the answers as you work on each question.

You should study the solutions to the answers in the first practice test carefully, in addition to paying special attention to the exam tips, which are highlighted in the "A+" boxes.

When you have studied the tips and sample problems, you should then do the remaining practice tests in the book.

The answers and explanations to practice tests 2 to 5 are provided after practice test 5.

TABLE OF CONTENTS

HESI Math Practice Test 1 with Math Concept Review:

Computations with Integers	1
Decimal Operations	3
Fractions: Multiplying Fractions	4
- Dividing Fractions	4
- Finding the Lowest Common Denominator (LCD)	5
- Simplifying Fractions	7
Mixed Numbers	9
Measurements and the Metric System	11
Military Time	12
PEMDAS – Order of Operations	14
Percentages and Decimals	15
Place Value	17
Proportions	18
Ratios	19
Remainders	20
Temperature	21
Working with Averages	22

Algebra concepts and formulas:

Substituting Values in Expressions	24
Solving for an Unknown Variable	24
Setting Up Basic Equations	25

Additional Practice Tests:

HESI Math Practice Test 2	28
HESI Math Practice Test 3	33
HESI Math Practice Test 4	38

HESI Math Practice Test 5   44

Solutions and Explanations to HESI Math Practice Tests 2 to 5:

HESI Math Practice Test 2 – Solutions and Explanations   51

HESI Math Practice Test 3 – Solutions and Explanations   64

HESI Math Practice Test 4 – Solutions and Explanations   76

HESI Math Practice Test 5 – Solutions and Explanations   87

Answer Key Practice Tests 2 to 5   95

HESI Math Practice Test 1 with Math Concept Review

Computations with Integers

Computations with integers are assessed on the HESI examination.

Integers are positive and negative whole numbers. Integers cannot have decimals, nor can they be mixed numbers. In other words, they can't contain fractions.

One of the most important concepts to remember about integers is that two negative signs together make a positive number.

Why do two negatives make a positive? In plain English, you can think of it like using "not" two times in one sentence.

For example, you tell your friend: "I do not want you to not go to the party."

In the sentence above, you are really telling your friend that you want him or her to attend the party.

In other words, the "two negatives" concept in math is similar to the "two negatives" concept in the English language.

So, when you see a number like $-(-2)$ you have to use 2 in your calculation.

Look at the example problem that follows.

Problem 1:

$-(-5) + 3 = ?$

A. -8

B. -2

C. 2

D. 8

The correct answer is D.

According to the concepts stated above, we know that $-(-5) = 5$

So, we can substitute this into the equation in order to solve it.

− (−5) + 3 = ?

5 + 3 = 8

 Remember that when you see two negatives signs together, you need to make a positive number.

You will also see problems that ask you to perform multiplication or division on integers. Some of these problems may ask you to find an integer that meets certain mathematical requirements, like in problem 2 below.

Problem 2:

What is the largest possible product of two even integers whose sum is 22?

A. 11

B. 44

C. 100

D. 120

The correct answer is D.

For problems that ask you to find the largest possible product of two even integers, first you need to divide the sum by 2.

The sum in this problem is 22, so we need to divide this by 2.

22 ÷ 2 = 11

Now take the result from this division and find the 2 nearest even integers that are 1 number higher and lower.

11 + 1 = 12

11 − 1 = 10

Then multiply these two numbers together in order to get the product.

12 × 10 = 120

Decimal Operations

You will see questions on the test that ask you to add or subtract decimal numbers.

Line up all of the numbers by the decimal points before you perform the operations.

> Line up the decimal points when you add up, as shown below. Then remember to carry the 1 if needed.
>
> 4.2500
> 0.0030
> 0.0148
> ?

Problem:

4.25 + 0.003 + 0.148 = ?

A. 4.401

B. 4.428

C. 5.76

D. 44.01

The correct answer is A.

Line up the decimal points as shown when adding. You can add in extra zeroes at the end of each number as placeholders.

Always remember to "carry the 1."

```
 11
4.250
0.003
0.148
4.401
```

Fractions – Multiplying

You will see problems on the exam that ask you to multiply fractions.

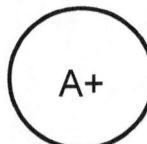

When multiplying fractions, multiply the numerators from each fraction. Then multiply the denominators.

The numerator is the number on the top of each fraction.

The denominator is the number on the bottom of the fraction.

Problem:

What is $\frac{1}{3} \times \frac{2}{3}$?

A. $\frac{2}{3}$

B. $\frac{2}{6}$

C. $\frac{2}{9}$

D. $\frac{1}{3}$

The correct answer is C.

Multiply the numerators.

$1 \times 2 = 2$

Then multiply the denominators.

$3 \times 3 = 9$

These numbers form the new fraction.

$\frac{2}{9}$

Fractions – Dividing

You will also need to know how to divide fractions for the exam.

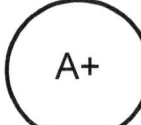

To divide fractions, invert the second fraction by putting the denominator on the top and numerator on the bottom. Then multiply.

Problem:

$\frac{1}{5} \div \frac{4}{7} = ?$

A. $\frac{4}{20}$

B. $\frac{7}{20}$

C. $\frac{4}{35}$

D. $\frac{5}{35}$

The correct answer is B.

Remember to invert the second fraction by putting the denominator on the top and the numerator on the bottom.

Our problem was: $\frac{1}{5} \div \frac{4}{7} = ?$

So the second fraction $\frac{4}{7}$ becomes $\frac{7}{4}$ when inverted.

Now use the inverted fraction to solve the problem.

$\frac{1}{5} \div \frac{4}{7} =$

$\frac{1}{5} \times \frac{7}{4} = \frac{1 \times 7}{5 \times 4} = \frac{7}{20}$

Fractions – Finding the Lowest Common Denominator (LCD)

In some fraction problems, you will have to find the lowest common denominator.

In other words, before you add or subtract fractions, you have to change them so that the bottom numbers in each fraction are the same. You do this by multiplying the numerator [top number] by the same number you use on the denominator for each fraction.

A+ Remember to multiply the numerator and denominator by the same number when you are converting to the LCD.

Problem:

What is $1/9 + 9/27$?

A. $12/27$

B. $9/27$

C. $3/27$

D. $10/36$

The correct answer is A.

STEP 1: To find the LCD, you have to look at the factors for each denominator.

Factors are the numbers that equal a product when they are multiplied by each other.

So, the factors of 9 are:

1 × 9 = 9

3 × 3 = 9

The factors of 27 are:

1 × 27 = 27

3 × 9 = 27

STEP 2: Determine which factors are common to both denominators by comparing the lists of factors.

In this problem, the factors of 3 and 9 are common to the denominators of both fractions.

We can illustrate the common factors as shown.

We saw that the factors of 9 were:

1 × **9** = 9

3 × 3 = 9

The factors of 27 were:

1 × 27 = 27

3 × **9** = 27

So, the numbers in bold above are the common factors.

STEP 3: Multiply the common factors to get the lowest common denominator.

The numbers that are in bold above are then used to calculate the lowest common denominator.

3 × 9 = 27

So, the lowest common denominator (LCD) for each fraction above is 27.

STEP 4: Convert the denominator of each fraction to the LCD.

You convert the fraction by referring to the factors from step 3.

Multiply the numerator and the denominator by the same factor.

Our problem was $1/9 + 9/27$.

So, we convert the first fraction as follows:

$1/9 \times 3/3 = 3/27$

We do not need to convert the second fraction of $9/27$ because it already has the LCD.

STEP 5: When both fractions have the same denominator, you can perform the operation to solve the problem.

$3/27 + 9/27 = 12/27$

Fractions – Simplifying

You will also need to know how to simplify fractions.

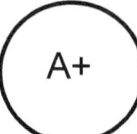

To simplify fractions, look to see what factors are common to both the numerator and denominator.

In the example problem above, our result was $^{12}/_{27}$.

Problem:

Simplify: $^{12}/_{27}$

A. $^{1}/_{3}$

B. $^{3}/_{4}$

C. $^{3}/_{9}$

D. $^{4}/_{9}$

The correct answer is D.

STEP 1: Look at the factors of the numerator and denominator.

The factors of 12 are:

1 × 12 = 12

2 × 6 = 12

3 × **4** = 12

You will remember that the factors of 27 are:

1 × 27 = 27

3 × 9 = 27

So, we can see that the numerator and denominator have the common factor of 3.

STEP 2: Simplify the fraction by dividing the numerator and denominator by the common factor.

Our fraction in this problem is $^{12}/_{27}$.

So, simplify the numerator: 12 ÷ 3 = 4

Then simplify the denominator: 27 ÷ 3 = 9

STEP 3: Use the results from step 2 to form the new fraction.

The numerator from step 2 is 4.

The denominator is 9.

So, the new fraction is ⁴/₉.

Mixed Numbers

Mixed numbers are those that contain a whole number and a fraction.

Convert the mixed numbers back to fractions first. Then find the lowest common denominator of the fractions in order to solve the problem.

Problem:

$$3\frac{1}{3} - 2\frac{1}{2} = ?$$

A. $\frac{1}{3}$

B. $\frac{9}{3}$

C. $\frac{5}{6}$

D. $1\frac{1}{2}$

The correct answer is C.

Our problem was: $3\frac{1}{3} - 2\frac{1}{2} = ?$

STEP 1: Convert the first mixed number to an integer plus a fraction.

$$3\frac{1}{3} = 3 + \frac{1}{3}$$

STEP 2: Then multiply the integer by a fraction whose numerator and denominator are the same as the denominator of the existing fraction.

$$3 + \frac{1}{3} =$$

$$\left(3 \times \frac{3}{3}\right) + \frac{1}{3} =$$

$$\frac{9}{3} + \frac{1}{3}$$

STEP 3: Add the two fractions to get your new fraction.

$$\frac{9}{3} + \frac{1}{3} = \frac{10}{3}$$

Then convert the second mixed number to a fraction, using the same steps that we have just completed for the first mixed number.

$$2\frac{1}{2} = 2 + \frac{1}{2} =$$

$$\left(2 \times \frac{2}{2}\right) + \frac{1}{2} =$$

$$\frac{4}{2} + \frac{1}{2} = \frac{5}{2}$$

Now that you have converted both mixed numbers to fractions, find the lowest common denominator and subtract to solve.

$$\frac{10}{3} - \frac{5}{2} =$$

$$\left(\frac{10}{3} \times \frac{2}{2}\right) - \left(\frac{5}{2} \times \frac{3}{3}\right) =$$

$$\frac{20}{6} - \frac{15}{6} = \frac{5}{6}$$

Measurements and the Metric System

Be sure to know the following conversions for your exam.

Weights:

1 gram = 0.035 ounces

1 gram = 1,000 milligrams

1 gram = 0.001 kilogram

1 ounce = 28.35 grams

1 pound = 453.59 grams

1 pound = 0.45 kilograms

1 kilogram = 1,000 grams

1 kilogram = 2.2 pounds

1 ton = 2,000 pounds

1 pound = 16 ounces

Liquid Measurements:

1 ounce = 30 milliliters

1 cup = 8 ounces

1 pint = 2 cups

1 pint = 16 ounces

1 quart = 2 pints

1 gallon = 4 quarts

1 gallon = 128 ounces

1 milliliter = 0.001 liter

1 milliliter = 0.035 ounce

1 liter = 1,000 milliliters

1 liter = 33.8 ounces

Length:

1 foot = 12 inches

1 yard = 3 feet

1 mile = 5,280 feet

1 mile = 1,760 yards

1 inch = 2.54 cm

1 millimeter (mm) = 0.1 centimeter (cm)

1 centimeter (cm) = 0.394 inch

1 centimeter (cm) = 0.01 meter

1 centimeter (cm) = 10 millimeters (mm)

1 meter = 100 centimeters

1 meter = 0.001 kilometer

1 kilometer = 1,000 meters

Military Time

Regular time uses AM for the morning and PM for times after noon.

Military time uses a 24 hour clock, with the numbers 00 to 23 representing the hours.

Minutes and seconds in military time are expressed the same way as in regular time.

To convert regular time to military time, put a zero before regular time for times before 10 AM.

Example: 8:32 AM = 0832 military time.

For times at or after 10 AM, add 12 to the hours (the number before the colon) in regular time.

Example: 5:28 PM = (5 +12) hours and 28 minutes = 17 hours and 28 minutes = 1728 military time

If you find the above calculations difficult, please study the following chart:

Regular Time	Military Time	Regular Time	Military Time
12:00 AM (midnight)	0000	12:00 PM (Noon)	1200
1:00 AM	0100	1:00 PM	1300
2:00 AM	0200	2:00 PM	1400
3:00 AM	0300	3:00 PM	1500
4:00 AM	0400	4:00 PM	1600
5:00 AM	0500	5:00 PM	1700
6:00 AM	0600	6:00 PM	1800
7:00 AM	0700	7:00 PM	1900
8:00 AM	0800	8:00 PM	2000
9:00 AM	0900	9:00 PM	2100
10:00 AM	1000	10:00 PM	2200
11:00 AM	1100	11:00 PM	2300

Problem:

What is 7:26 PM in military time?

A. 726

B. 0726

C. 1726

D. 1926

The correct answer is D.

Solve using the steps shown above:

7:26 PM =

7 + 12 hours and 26 minutes =

19 hours and 26 minutes =

1926 military time

PEMDAS – Order of Operations

The phrase "order of operations" means that you need to know which mathematical operation to do first when you are faced with longer problems.

Remember the acronym PEMDAS. "PEMDAS" means that you have to do the mathematical operations in this order:

First: Do operations inside **P**arentheses

Second: Do operations with **E**xponents

Third: Perform **M**ultiplication and **D**ivision (from left to right)

Last: Do **A**ddition and **S**ubtraction (from left to right)

Some students prefer to remember the order or operations by using the memorable phrase:

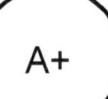

Please Excuse My Dear Aunt Sally

So, refer to the rules above and attempt the example problems that follow.

Problem 1:

$-6 \times 3 - 4 \div 2 = ?$

A. −20

B. −18

C. −2

D. 4

The correct answer is A.

There are no parentheses or exponents in this problem, so we need to direct our attention to the multiplication and division first.

Our problem was: $-6 \times 3 - 4 \div 2 = ?$

When you see a problem like this one, you need to do the multiplication and division from left to right.

This means that you take the number to the left of the multiplication or division symbol and multiply or divide that number on the left by the number on the right of the symbol.

So, in our problem we need to multiply –6 by 3 and then divide 4 by 2.

You can see the order of operations more clearly if you put in parentheses to group the numbers together.

$-6 \times 3 - 4 \div 2 =$

$(-6 \times 3) - (4 \div 2) =$

$-18 - 2 =$

-20

Percentages and Decimals

You will have to calculate percentages and decimals on the exam, as well as use percentages and decimals to solve other types of math problems or to create equations.

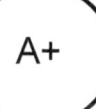 Percentages can be expressed by using the symbol %. They can also be expressed as fractions or decimals.

In general, there are three ways to express percentages.

TYPE 1: Percentages as fractions

Percentages can always be expressed as the number over one hundred.

So $45\% = {}^{45}/_{100}$

TYPE 2: Percentages as simplified fractions

Percentages can also be expressed as simplified fractions.

In order to simplify the fraction, you have to find the largest number that will go into both the numerator and denominator.

In the case of 45%, the fraction is $^{45}/_{100}$, and the numerator and denominator are both divisible by 5.

To simplify the numerator: $45 \div 5 = 9$.

To simplify the denominator: $100 \div 5 = 20$.

This results in the simplified fraction of $^{9}/_{20}$.

TYPE 3: Percentages as decimals

Percentages can also be expressed as decimals.

$45\% = {^{45}/_{100}} = 45 \div 100 = 0.45$

You may have to use these concepts in order to solve a practical problem, like the one that follows.

Problem:

Consider a class which has n students. In this class, $t\%$ of the students subscribe to digital TV packages.

Which of the following represents the number of students who do not subscribe to any digital TV package?

A. $100(n - t)$

B. $(100\% - t\%) \times n$

C. $(100\% - t\%) \div n$

D. $(1 - t)n$

The correct answer is B.

If $t\%$ subscribe to digital TV packages, then $100\% - t\%$ do not subscribe.

In other words, since a percentage is any given number out of 100%, the percentage of students who do not subscribe is represented by this equation:

$(100\% - t\%)$

This equation is then multiplied by the total number of students (n) in order to determine the number of students who do not subscribe to digital TV packages.

$(100\% - t\%) \times n$

Place Value

These following two questions assess your understanding of decimal place value.

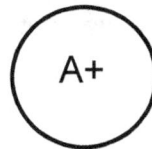

Remember that the number after the decimal is in the tenths place.
The second number after the decimal is in the hundredths place.
The third number after the decimal is in the thousandths place.
The fourth number after the decimal is in the ten thousandths place.

What is 0.96547 rounded to the nearest thousandth?

A. 0.96

B. 0.97

C. 0.965

D. 0.966

The correct answer is C.

The thousandths place is the third one to the right of the decimal.

So, 0.96547 rounded to the nearest thousandth is 0.965

Problem 2:

When 1523.48 is divided by 100, which digit of the resulting number is in the tenths place?

A. 1

B. 2

C. 3

D. 4

The correct answer is B.

Perform the division, and then check the decimal places of the numbers.

Divide as follows: 1523.48 ÷ 100 = 15.2348

Reading our result from left to right: 1 is in the tens place, 5 is in the ones place, 2 is in the tenths place, 3 is in the hundredths place, 4 is in the thousandths place, and 8 is in the ten-thousandths place.

Proportions

A proportion is an equation with a ratio on each side. In other words, a proportion is a statement that two ratios are equal. $3/4 = 6/8$ is an example of a proportion.

We will look at ratios in more depth in the next section.

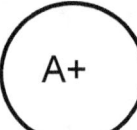

| Proportions often involve simplifying fractions, which we have learned how to do in a previous section. |

Proportions can be expressed as fractions, as in the following problem.

Problem:

Find the value of x that solves the following proportion: $3/6 = x/14$

A. 3

B. 6

C. 7

D. 9

The correct answer is C.

STEP 1: You can simplify the first fraction because both the numerator and denominator are divisible by 3.

$3/6 \div 3/3 = 1/2$

STEP 2: Then divide the denominator of the second fraction ($x/14$) by the denominator of the simplified fraction ($1/2$) from above.

14 ÷ 2 = 7

STEP 3: Now, multiply the number from step 2 by the numerator of the fraction we calculated in step 1 in order to get your result.

1 × 7 = 7

You can check your answer by simplifying each fraction as follows:

$3/6 = 7/14$

$3/6 \div 3/3 = 1/2$

$7/14 \div 7/7 = 1/2$

Ratios

Ratios take a group of people or things and divide them into two parts.

For example, if your teacher tells you that each day you should spend two hours studying math for every hour that you spend studying English, you get the ratio 2:1.

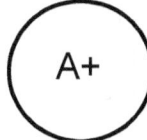 Ratios can be expressed as fractions. Ratios can also be expressed by using the colon. For example, a ratio of 2 to 100 can be expressed as $2/100$ or 2:100.

The number before the colon expresses one subset of the total amount of items. The number after the colon expresses a different subset of the total. In other words, when the number before the colon and the number after the colon are added together, we have the total amount of items.

Problem:

In a shipment of 100 mp3 players, 1% are faulty.

What is the ratio of non-faulty mp3 players to faulty mp3 players?

A. 99:1

B. 99:100

C. 1:99

D. 1:100

The correct answer is A.

This problem is asking for the quantity of non-faulty mp3 players to the quantity of faulty mp3 players.

Therefore, you must put the quantity of non-faulty mp3 players before the colon in the ratio.

In this problem, 1% of the players are faulty.

1% × 100 = 1 faulty player in every 100 players

100 − 1 = 99 non-faulty players

As explained above, the number before the colon and the number after the colon can be added together to get the total quantity.

So, the ratio is 99:1.

Remainders

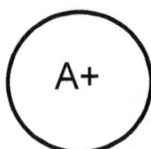 The remainder is the amount that is left over after you divide into whole numbers. These whole numbers are referred to as factors. So, ask yourself what products can be calculated by multiplying another number by 3: 1 × 3 = 3; 2 × 3 = 6; 3 × 3 = 9; 4 × 3 = 12 and so on.

What is the remainder when 11 is divided by 3?

A. 0.66

B. 0.67

C. 2

D. 3

The correct answer is C.

Determine which numbers can be calculated by multiplying another integer by 3:

1 × 3 = 3

2 × 3 = 6

3 × 3 = 9

4 × 3 = 12

12 is greater than 11, so the nearest product to 11 from the list above is 9.

We subtract these two numbers to get the remainder: 11 − 9 = 2

Temperature

You may need to change temperature from Celsius to Fahrenheit or from Fahrenheit to Celsius for your exam.

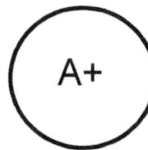

Use the following formula to convert from Fahrenheit to Celsius:
°C = 0.56(°F − 32)
Use this formula to convert from Celsius to Fahrenheit:
°F = 1.8(°C) + 32

Problem:

Express in Celsius: 96° F

A. 35.84

B. 64.00

C. 172.8

D. 204.8

The correct answer is A.

We are converting from Fahrenheit to Celsius, so use the first formula from above:

°C = 0.56(°F − 32)

Start with the degrees F and subtract 32: 96 − 32 = 64

Multiply the result from the first step by 0.56: 0.56 × 64 = 35.84

Working with Averages

Basic averages are calculated by taking the total of a data set for a group and then dividing this total by the number of people in the group.

For example, have a look at the following problem.

Three people are trying to lose weight. The first person has lost 7 pounds, the second person has lost 10 pounds, and the third person has lost 16 pounds. What is the average weight loss for this group?

STEP 1: Add all of the individual amounts together to get a total for the group.

7 + 10 + 16 = 33

STEP 2: Divide the total from step 1 by the number of people in the group.

33 ÷ 3 = 11

So, the average weight loss is 11 pounds.

However, problems with averages on the HESI Test might be more difficult than the one provided above.

Problems that you see on the exam might involve an average that was calculated in error.

To solve, find the total of the data set by reversing the erroneous operation.

Then divide the total by the correct number of items in order to find the correct average.

Other types of problems will give you averages for two distinct members of a group, like male and female students in a class, and then ask you to calculate the average for the entire group.

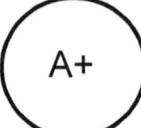

For advanced problems on averages, multiply each average by the number of people in each group. Then add the totals for each group together and divide by the total number of people.

Problem:

120 students took a math test. The 60 female students in the class had an average score of 95, while the 60 male students in the class had an average of 90. What is the average test score for all 120 students in the class?

A. 75

B. 92.5

C. 93

D. 93.5

The correct answer is B.

STEP 1: You need to find the total points for all the females by multiplying their average by the number of female students. Then do the same to find the total points for all the males.

Females: 60 × 95 = 5700

Males: 60 × 90 = 5400

STEP 2: Then add these two amounts together to get the total for the group.

5700 + 5400 = 11,100

STEP 3: Then divide by the total number of students in the class to get your solution.

11,100 ÷ 120 = 92.5

So, the correct average is 92.5.

Algebra concepts and formulas

Substituting Values in Algebraic Expressions

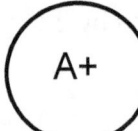

You may be asked to calculate the value of an expression by substituting its values. To solve these problems, put in the values for x and y and multiply. Then do the addition and subtraction.

Problem:

What is the value of the expression $4x^2 + 2xy - y^2$ when $x = 2$ and $y = -2$?

A. 4

B. 6

C. 8

D. 12

The correct answer is A.

$4x^2 + 2xy - y^2 =$

$(4 \times 2^2) + (2 \times 2 \times -2) - (-2^2) =$

$(4 \times 2 \times 2) + (2 \times 2 \times -2) - (-2 \times -2) =$

$(4 \times 4) + (2 \times -4) - (4) =$

$16 + (-8) - 4 =$

$16 - 12 = 4$

Solving for an Unknown Variable

You will see problems involving solving equations for an unknown variable on the exam.

Perform the multiplication on the items in parentheses first. Then eliminate the integers and solve for x.

If $3x - 2(x + 5) = -8$, then $x = ?$

A. 1

B. 2

C. 3

D. 5

The correct answer is B.

To solve this type of problem, do multiplication on the items in parentheses first.

$3x - 2(x + 5) = -8$

$3x - 2x - 10 = -8$

Then deal with the integers by putting them on one side of the equation.

$3x - 2x - 10 + 10 = -8 + 10$

$3x - 2x = 2$

Then solve for x.

$3x - 2x = 2$

$1x = 2$

$x = 2$

Setting Up Basic Equations

You may see problems on the test that ask you to make mathematical equations from basic information.

To set up an equation, read the problem carefully and then express the facts in terms of an algebraic equation.

These types of questions are often practical problems that involve buying or selling merchandise.

Problem 1:

A company purchases cell phones at a cost of x and sells the cell phones at four times the cost. Which of the following represents the profit made on each cell phone?

A. x

B. 3x

C. 4x

D. 3 − x

The correct answer is B.

The sales price of each cell phone is four times the cost.

The cost is expressed as x, so the sales price is 4x.

The difference between the sales price of each cell phone and the cost of each cell phone is the profit.

REMEMBER: Sales Price − Cost = Profit

In this problem, the sales price is 4x and the cost is x.

4x − x = Profit

3x = Profit

Problem 2:

An internet provider sells internet packages based on monthly rates. The price for the internet service depends on the speed of the internet connection.

The prices of the various internet packages are as follows:

Price in Dollars: $10 $20 $30 $40

Speed in GB: 2   4   6   8

Which equation represents the prices of these internet packages?

A. $P = (s - 5) \times 5$

B. $P = (s + 5) \times 5$

C. $P = 5 \div s$

D. $P = s \times 5$

The correct answer is D.

The price of the internet connection is always 5 times the speed.

$10 = 2 \times 5$

$20 = 4 \times 5$

$30 = 6 \times 5$

$40 = 8 \times 5$

So, the price of the internet connection (represented by variable P) equals the speed (represented by variable s) times 5.

$P = s \times 5$

HESI Math Practice Test 2:

1) Evaluate: $2x^2 - x + 5$ if $x = -2$

2) Solve for x: $-6x + 5 = -19$

3) An infant weighs 12 pounds 4 ounces. What is the infant's weight in grams?

4) What temperature in Fahrenheit is equivalent to 35° Celsius?

5) A health care professional works from 1800 to 0200. How many hours has she worked?

6) How many ounces are there in one liter?

7) How many milliliters are there in one liter?

8) How many centimeters are there in one meter?

9) 4 quarts = _____ ounces

10) A newborn measures 53 cm in length. How long is the newborn in inches?

11) Two people are going to give money to a foundation for a project. Person A will provide one-half of the money. Person B will donate one-eighth of the money. What fraction represents the unfunded portion of the project?
A) $1/16$
B) $1/8$
C) $1/4$
D) $3/8$

12) A hockey team had 50 games this season and lost 20 percent of them. How many games did the team win?
A) 8
B) 10
C) 20
D) 40

13) Carmen wanted to find the average of the five tests she has taken this semester. However, she erroneously divided the total points from the five tests by 4, which gave her a result of 90. What is the correct average of her five tests?
A) 64
B) 72
C) 80
D) 90

14) Beth took a test that had 60 questions. She got 10% of her answers wrong. How many questions did she answer correctly?
   A) 6
   B) 10
   C) 50
   D) 54

15) Professor Smith uses a system of extra-credit points for his class. Extra-credit points can be offset against the points lost on an exam due to incorrect responses. David answered 18 questions incorrectly on the exam and lost 36 points. He then earned 25 extra credit points. By how much was his exam score ultimately lowered?
   A) –11
   B) 11
   C) 18
   D) 25

16) A group of friends are trying to lose weight. Person A lost $14^{3}/_{4}$ pounds. Person B lost $20^{1}/_{5}$ pounds. Person C lost 36.35 pounds. What is the total weight loss for the group?
   A) 70.475
   B) 71.05
   C) 71.15
   D) 71.30

17) A job is shared by 4 workers, A, B, C, and D. Worker A does $^{1}/_{6}$ of the total hours. Worker B does $^{1}/_{3}$ of the total hours. Worker C does $^{1}/_{6}$ of the total hours. What fraction represents the remaining hours allocated to person D?
   A) $^{1}/_{8}$
   B) $^{3}/_{8}$
   C) $^{1}/_{6}$
   D) $^{1}/_{3}$

18) The university bookstore is having a sale. Course books can be purchased for $40 each, or 5 books can be purchased for a total of $150. How much would a student save on each book if he or she purchased 5 books?
   A) 5
   B) 10
   C) 50
   D) 90

19) One hundred students took an English test. The 55 female students in the class had an average score of 87, while the 45 male students in the class had an average of 80. What is the average test score for all 100 students in the class?
   A) 82.00
   B) 83.15
   C) 83.50
   D) 83.85

20) Mary needs to get $650 in donations. So far, she has obtained 80% of the money she needs. How much money does she still need?
   A) $8.19
   B) $13.00
   C) $32.50
   D) $130.00

21) If $5x - 2(x + 3) = 0$, then $x = ?$
   A) –2
   B) –1
   C) 1
   D) 2

22) What is the value of the expression $6x^2 - xy + y^2$ when $x = 5$ and $y = -1$?
   A) 36
   B) 144
   C) 146
   D) 156

23) Two people are going to work on a job. The first person will be paid $7.25 per hour. The second person will be paid $10.50 per hour. If A represents the number of hours the first person will work, and B represents the number of hours the second person will work, what equation represents the total cost of the wages for this job?
   A) 17.75AB
   B) 17.75 ÷ AB
   C) AB ÷ 17.75
   D) (7.25A + 10.50B)

24) Mark's final grade for a course is based on the grades from two tests, A and B. Test A counts toward 35% of his final grade. Test B counts toward 65% of his final grade. What equation is used to calculate Mark's final grade for this course?
   A) 0.65A + 0.35B
   B) 0.35A + 0.65B
   C) (0.35A + 0.65B) ÷ 2
   D) A + B

25) Find the value of x that solves the following proportion: $3/9 = x/21$
   A) 3
   B) 6
   C) 7
   D) 8

26) $33.3 \times 2.5 = ?$

27) The Jones family needs to dig a new well. The well will be 525 feet deep, and it will be topped with a windmill which will be 95 feet in height. What is the distance from the deepest point of the well to the top of the windmill?
   A) 95 feet
   B) 430 feet
   C) 525 feet
   D) 620 feet

28) Mrs. Janowsky is having a birthday party for her son. She is going to give balloons to the children. She has one bag that contains 13 balloons, another that contains 22 balloons, and a third that contains 25 balloons. If 12 children are going to attend the party including her son, and the total amount of balloons is to be divided equally among all of the children, how many balloons will each child receive?
   A) 3
   B) 4
   C) 5
   D) 6

29) A bookstore is offering a 15% discount on books. Janet's purchase would be $90 at the normal price. How much will she pay after the discount?
   A) $75.50
   B) $76.50
   C) $77.50
   D) $85.50

30) John is measuring plant growth as part of a botany experiment. Last week, his plant grew 7¾ inches, but this week his plant grew 10½ inches. What is the difference in growth in inches between the two weeks?
   A) 2¼ inches
   B) 2½ inches
   C) 2¾ inches
   D) 3¼ inches

31) Patty works 23 hours a week at a part-time job for which she receives $7.50 an hour. She then gets a raise, after which she earns $184 per week. She continues to work 23 hours per week. How much did her hourly pay increase?
   A) 50 cents an hour
   B) 75 cents an hour
   C) $1.00 an hour
   D) $8.00 an hour

32) Sheng Li is driving at 70 miles per hour. At 10:00 am, he sees a sign that reads as follows:

Washington	140 miles
Yorkville	105 miles
Zorster	210 miles

He continues driving at the same speed. Where will Sheng Li be at 11:00 am?
A) 70 miles from Washington
B) 105 miles from Washington
C) 75 miles from Yorkville
D) 80 miles from Yorkville

33) Mayumi spent the day counting cars for her job as a traffic controller. In the morning she counted 114 more cars than she did in the afternoon. If she counted 300 cars in total that day, how many cars did she count in the morning?
A) 90
B) 93
C) 114
D) 207

34) Tiffany buys five pairs of socks for $2.50 each. The next day, she decides to exchange these five pairs of socks for four different pairs that cost $3 each. She uses this equation to calculate her refund: (5 × $2.50) – (4 × $3). Which equation below could she have used instead?
A) (5 × 4) – (3 × 2.50)
B) $2.50 – 4($3 – $2.50)
C) (5 × 4) + (3 × 2.50)
D) $3 – (4 × $2.50)

35) Mr. Carlson needs to calculate 35% of 90. To do so, he uses the following equation:

$$\frac{35 \times 90}{100}$$

Which of the following could he also have used?
A) (35 × 90) ÷ 100
B) (35 ÷ 90) × 100
C) (35 – 90) × 100
D) 90 × 0.0035

36) Use the table below to answer the question that follows.

Waterloo Station Bus Timetable	
Departure Time	Arrival Time
9:18 am	11:06 am
10:32 am	12:20 pm
11:52 am	?
1:03 pm	2:51 pm

The bus journeys from Waterloo Station to a nearby town are always the same duration. What time is missing from the above timetable?
A) 12:40 pm
B) 1:34 pm
C) 1:40 pm
D) 1:48 pm

37) Item C costs 20% more per pound than item B. If a 12 pound container of item B costs $48, what is the cost per pound of item C?
A) $4.12
B) $4.20
C) $4.60
D) $4.80

38) The cost of a photography course is $20 per week plus a $5 fee per week for review of photographs and administration. What is the total cost of the course and fees for W weeks?
A) $20W
B) $25W
C) $20 + 5W
D) $5 + 20W

39) Add: 7 + 13.45 + 6.028 = ?

40) Subtract: 32.7 − 6.25 = ?

HESI Math Practice Test 3:

1) Evaluate: $3x^2 + 2x + 7$ if $x = -3$

2) Solve for x: $3x + 5 = -22$

3) A patient's height is 65 inches. How tall is the patient in centimeters?

4) What temperature in Celsius is equivalent to 99° Fahrenheit?

5) A nurse's usual shift is from 0000 to 0800. What time of day does he work?
A) 8 AM to midnight
B) noon to 8 AM
C) noon to 8 PM
D) midnight to 8 AM

6) How many pounds are there in one kilogram?

7) How many millimeters are there in one centimeter?

8) What conversion factor is used to convert meters to centimeters?

9) 2 pints = _____ milliliters

10) A piece of surgical equipment weighs 12,538 grams. What is the weight in kilograms?

11) − (−6) + 2 = ?

A) −8
B) −4
C) 4
D) 8

12) $\frac{1}{5} \times \frac{2}{3} = ?$

    A) $\frac{1}{4}$
    B) $\frac{3}{8}$
    C) $\frac{2}{15}$
    D) $\frac{10}{3}$

13) $\frac{4}{7} \div \frac{2}{3} = ?$

    A) $\frac{8}{21}$
    B) $\frac{12}{14}$
    C) $\frac{6}{8}$
    D) $\frac{14}{12}$

14) $\frac{1}{8} + \frac{3}{16} = ?$

    A) $\frac{5}{16}$
    B) $\frac{4}{24}$
    C) $\frac{16}{5}$
    D) $\frac{24}{16}$

15) Simplify: $\frac{12}{14}$

    A) $\frac{1}{7}$
    B) $\frac{4}{7}$
    C) $\frac{7}{6}$
    D) $\frac{6}{7}$

16) $4\frac{1}{8} - 3\frac{5}{6} = ?$

   A) $-1\frac{1}{2}$

   B) $1\frac{17}{24}$

   C) $\frac{7}{24}$

   D) $\frac{24}{7}$

17) $-5 \times 4 - 6 \div 3 = ?$

   A) -22

   B) $-\frac{26}{3}$

   C) -18

   D) $\frac{10}{3}$

18) The price of a certain book is reduced from $60 to $45 at the end of the semester. By what percent is the price of the book reduced?
   A) 15%
   B) 20%
   C) 25%
   D) 33%

19) The price of socks is $2 per pair and the price of shoes is $25 per pair. Anna went shopping for socks and shoes, and she paid $85 in total. In this purchase, she bought 3 pairs of shoes. How many pairs of socks did she buy?
   A) 2
   B) 3
   C) 5
   D) 8

20) The Smith family is having lunch in a diner. They buy hot dogs and hamburgers to eat. The hot dogs cost $2.50 each, and the hamburgers cost $4 each. They buy 3 hamburgers. They also buy hot dogs. The total value of their purchase is $22. How many hot dogs did they buy?
   A) 3
   B) 4
   C) 5
   D) 6

21) At the beginning of class, $^1/_5$ of the students leave to go to singing lessons. Then $^1/_4$ of the remaining students leave to go to the principal's office. If 18 students are then left in the class, how many students were there at the beginning of class?
   A) 90
   B) 45
   C) 30
   D) 25

22) A dance academy had 300 students at the beginning of January. It lost 5% of its students during the month. However, 15 new students joined the academy on the last day of the month. If this pattern continues for the next two months, how many students will there be at the academy at the end of March?
   A) 285
   B) 300
   C) 310
   D) 315

23) The price of a wool coat is reduced 12.5% at the end of the winter. If the original price of the coat was $120, what will the price be after the reduction?
   A) $108.00
   B) $107.50
   C) $105.70
   D) $105.00

24) Yesterday a train traveled $117^3/_4$ miles. Today it traveled $102^1/_6$ miles. What is the difference between the distance traveled today and yesterday?
   A) 15 miles
   B) $15^1/_4$ miles
   C) $15^7/_{12}$ miles
   D) $15^9/_{12}$ miles

25) Sam is driving a truck at 70 miles per hour. At 10:30 am, he sees this sign:
   Brownsville   35 miles
   Dunnstun   70 miles
   Farnam   140 miles
   Georgetown   210 miles
   After Sam sees the sign, he continues to drive at the same speed. At 11:00 am, how far will he be from Farnam?
   A) He will be in Farnam.
   B) He will be 35 miles from Farnam.
   C) He will be 70 miles from Farnam.
   D) He will be 105 miles from Farnam.

26) In a math class, $1/3$ of the students fail a test. If twelve students have failed the test, how many students are in the class in total?
   A) 15
   B) 16
   C) 36
   D) 38

27) Mark owns a bargain bookstore that sells every book for $5. Last week, his sales were $525. This week his sales figure was $600. How many more books did Mark sell this week, compared to last week?
   A) 5
   B) 15
   C) 25
   D) 75

28) Kieko needs to calculate 16% of 825. Which of the following formulas can she use?
   A) 825×16
   B) 160×825
   C) 825×1600
   D) 825×0.16

29) Wei Lei bought a shirt on sale. The original price of the shirt was $18, and he got a 40% discount. What was the sales price of the shirt?
   A) $7.20
   B) $10.80
   C) $11.80
   D) $17.60

30) Professor Flores calculates students' grades for her course by taking the average of two exams, and then deducting 2 points from this average for every day a student misses class. You got 85 and 91 on the exams and you were absent 3 times. What is your grade for the course?
   A) 82
   B) 85
   C) 88
   D) 91

31) The county is proposing a 7.5% increase in its annual real estate tax. If the tax is currently $480 per year, how much would the tax be if the proposed increase is approved?
   A) $444
   B) $487
   C) $516
   D) $840

32) Mrs. Ramirez is inviting 12 children to her son's birthday party. The children will play pin the tail on the donkey. Mrs. Ramirez has already made 40 tails for the game. She wants to give each child 4 tails to play the game. How many more tails does she need to make?
   A) 4
   B) 8
   C) 10
   D) 12

33) A class contains 20 students. On Tuesday 5% of the students were absent. On Wednesday 20% of the students were absent. How many more students were absent on Wednesday than on Tuesday?
   A) 1
   B) 2
   C) 3
   D) 4

34) $x^2 + xy - y = 41$ and $x = 5$. What is the value of y?
   A) 2.6
   B) 4
   C) 6
   D) −4

35) If $4x - 3(x + 2) = -3$, then $x = ?$
   A) 9
   B) 3
   C) 1
   D) −3

36) Multiply: (8.2)(0.13)

37) Multiply: 425 × 2.5

38) Subtract: 12.013 − 0.14

39) Subtract: 14.9 − 7.2

40) Add: 35.2 + 8.015

HESI Math Practice Test 4:

1) Evaluate: $x^2 - 5x - 9$ if $x = 8$

2) Solve for x: $5x - 9 = 6$

3) A patient should be administered 0.7 grams of a certain medicine per week. How much medicine should be administered to the patient per week in milligrams?

4) What temperature in Fahrenheit is equivalent to 49° Celsius?

5) You must dilute a powder with 4 cups of water, but your measuring device is in ounces. How many ounces of liquid should you add to the powder?

6) 16 gallons = _____ quarts

7) You recommend that certain weight-loss patients should walk 21,000 feet per week. How many yards should they walk per day?

8) You need to order 200,000 milliliters of an intravenous drug, but the order form has to be filled out in pints and ounces. How many pints and ounces should you order?

9) How many yards are there in one mile?

10) You need to travel 500,000 meters to a conference. How many kilometers must you travel?

11) A class which has x students. s% of the students have been absent this semester. Which of the following equations represents the number of students who have not been absent this semester?
A) 100(s − x)
B) (100% − s%) × x
C) (100% − s%) ÷ x
D) (1 − s)x

12) What is 1,594 + 23,786?
A) 24,380
B) 25,380
C) 24.270
D) 25,270

13) A club has 25 members. If each member pays $15 in annual fees, how much money will the club collect in total for the membership fees?
A) $375
B) $355
C) $325
D) $295

14) Which of the following is the greatest?
   A) 0.350
   B) 0.035
   C) 0.053
   D) 0.3035

15) The total funds, represented by variable F, available for P charity projects is represented by the equation F = \$500P + \$3,700. If the charity has \$40,000 available for projects, what is the greatest number of complete projects that can be completed?
   A) 72
   B) 73
   C) 74
   D) 79

16) Which of the following shows the numbers ordered from greatest to least?
   A) $-1/3, 1/7, 1, 1/5$
   B) $-1/3, 1/7, 1/5, 1$
   C) $-1/3, 1, 1/7, 1/5$
   D) $1, 1/5, 1/7, -1/3$

17) During each flight, a flight attendant must count the number of passengers on board the aircraft. The morning flight had 52 passengers more than the evening flight, and there were 540 passengers in total on the two flights that day. How many passengers were there on the evening flight?
   A) 244
   B) 296
   C) 488
   D) 540

18) A cafeteria serves spaghetti to senior citizens on Fridays. The spaghetti comes prepared in large containers, and each container holds 15 servings of spaghetti. The cafeteria is expecting 82 senior citizens this Friday. What is the least number of containers of spaghetti that the cafeteria will need in order to serve all 82 people? It is not possible to purchase a partial container.
   A) 4
   B) 5
   C) 6
   D) 7

19) At the beginning of a class, one-fourth of the students leave to attend band practice. Later, one half of the remaining students leave to go to PE. If there were 15 students remaining in the class at the end, how many students were in the class at the beginning?
   A) 40
   B) 45
   C) 50
   D) 55

20) $82 + 9 \div 3 - 5 = ?$
   A) −40.50
   B) 40.50
   C) 80.00
   D) 85.33

21) $52 + 6 \times 3 - 48 = ?$
   A) 22
   B) 82
   C) 126
   D) 322

22) Convert the following to a decimal: $^4/_{16}$
   A) 0.0025
   B) 0.025
   C) 0.25
   D) 0.40

23) 90 is 30 percent of what number?
   A) 27
   B) 120
   C) 0.0375
   D) 300

24) $6^3/_4 - 2^1/_2 = ?$
   A) $4^1/_4$
   B) $4^3/_8$
   C) $4^5/_8$
   D) $4^6/_8$

25) 9 × 6 + 42 ÷ 6 = ?
   A) 8
   B) 16
   C) 27
   D) 61

26) The local Boy Scouts has 31 members. If each member contributes 12 cans of food for a food drive, how many cans of food are contributed in total?
   A) 472
   B) 372
   C) 132
   D) 43

27) $1/8 \div 4/3 = ?$
   A) $1/6$
   B) $32/3$
   C) $3/24$
   D) $3/32$

28) Convert the following fraction to decimal format: $5/50$
   A) 0.0010
   B) 0.0100
   C) 0.1000
   D) 0.0500

29) What is the remainder when 600 is divided by 9?
   A) 0.66
   B) 0.67
   C) 7
   D) 6

30) $3\frac{1}{2} - 2\frac{3}{5} = ?$
   A) $9/10$
   B) $1\frac{1}{10}$
   C) $1\frac{1}{3}$
   D) $1\frac{2}{3}$

31) The Abdul family is shopping at a superstore. They buy product A and product B. Product A costs $5 each, and product B costs $8 each. They buy 4 of product A. They also buy a certain quantity of product B. The total value of their purchase is $60. How many units of product B did they buy?
A) 4
B) 5
C) 6
D) 8

32) 3.75 + 0.162 = ?

33) Jonathan can run 3 miles in 25 minutes. If he maintains this pace, how long will it take him to run 12 miles?
A) 1 hour and 15 minutes
B) 1 hour and 40 minutes
C) 1 hour and 45 minutes
D) 3 hours

34) Mrs. Johnson is going to give candy to the students in her class. The first bag of candy that she has contains 43 pieces. The second contains 28 pieces, and the third contains 31 pieces. If there are 34 students in Mrs. Johnson's class, and the candy is divided equally among all of the students, how many pieces of candy will each student receive?
A) 3 pieces
B) 4 pieces
C) 5 pieces
D) 51 pieces

35) What is the value of the expression $2x^2 + 3xy - y^2$ when $x = 3$ and $y = -3$?
A) –18
B) 0
C) 18
D) 36

36) A recent survey shows that 50% of your patients rated your service as excellent and 25% rated your service as very good. What percentage represents the total amount of patients who rated your service either excellent or very good?
A) 25%
B) 50%
C) 75%
D) 85%

37) A patient has just requested 5 units of a nutritional product. Each unit of the product takes 1¼ hours to make. How much time is needed to make this order?
   A) 5 hours and 25 minutes
   B) 5 hours and 55 minutes
   C) 6 hours and 4 minutes
   D) 6 hours and 15 minutes

38) Multiply: (82)(0.17)

39) Subtract: 101.5 – 8.394

40) Add: 13.6 + 2.8

HESI Math Practice Test 5:

1) If $3x - 9 = -18$, then $x = ?$

2) Evaluate: $2x^2 + 8x$ if $x = 7$

3) How many ounces are there in one pound?

4) What temperature in Celsius is equivalent to 76° Fahrenheit?

5) Research indicates that many people are at least 14 pounds overweight. Indicate this amount in kilograms.

6) How many grams are there in one kilogram?

7) A nurse needs 0.75 liter of liquid suspension, but the order must be made in ounces. How many ounces should he order?

8) A patient has been in an accident and was hit by a car weighing 1.75 tons. What was the weight of the car in pounds?

9) 4 gallons = _____ ounces

10) How many inches are there in one mile?

11) A company sells electronics online. The annual sales for the first three years of business are: $25,135, $32,787, and $47,004. What were the total sales for the past three years?
   A) $101,326
   B) $104,916

C) $104,926
D) $104,944

12) A customer gives a cashier $50 to pay for the items purchased she purchased, which totaled $41.28. How much change should the cashier give the customer?
A) $7.82
B) $8.18
C) $8.27
D) $8.72

13) As car salesperson earns a $175 referral fee on every customer who accepts a customer service upgrade. He referred 8 customers for the service upgrade this month. How much did he earn in referral fees for the month?
A) $1050
B) $1200
C) $1225
D) $1400

14) Your weekly pay is $535.50 and you work 30 hours per week. How much are you paid per hour?
A) $17.83
B) $17.84
C) $17.85
D) $18.34

15) Business losses are represented as negative numbers, while business profits are represented as positive numbers. A business makes the following profits and losses during a four week period: −$286, $953, $1502, and −$107. What was the total business profit or loss during these four weeks?
A) $2,026
B) $2,062
C) $2,080
D) −$2,026

16) Location below sea level is represented as a negative number. The location below sea level of Lake Alto is −35 meters. The location below sea level of Lake Bajo is 62 meters deeper than Lake Alto. What figure represents the location below sea level for the Lake Bajo?
A) −97
B) 97
C) −62
D) −27

17) You are working on a project and have completed ³/₅ of it. What figure below expresses the project completion amount as a decimal number?
A) 0.06
B) 0.60
C) 1.67
D) 3.00

18) A teacher reports attendance as a decimal figure. This week, the attendance was 0.55. What percentage best represents the attendance for this week?
A) 0.55%
B) 5.50%
C) 55.0%
D) 55.5%

19) You have used up ⁵/₁₄ of your vacation days. Approximately what percentage of your vacation days have you already used?
A) 0.357%
B) 2.800%
C) 3.570%
D) 35.70%

20) You have used 0.75 of the gas you last put in your car. What fraction best represents the amount of gas you have used?
A) ¹/₄
B) ²/₅
C) ²/₃
D) ³/₄

21) It is reported that 33% of all new stores close within five years of opening. What fraction best represents this percentage?
A) ¹/₃
B) ¹/₄
C) ¹/₅
D) ²/₃

22) A carpet store is offering 45% off in a sale this month. What decimal number below best represents the percentage off?
A) 0.0045
B) 0.0450
C) 0.4500
D) 4.5000

23) A bakery has to pay 36 cents for each pound of flour it buys. It decides to by $14^{1}/_{4}$ pounds of flour today. How much will the bakery have to pay?
   A) $3.60
   B) $5.13
   C) $5.31
   D) $14.25

24) A bookkeeper has just been with a client for 0.35 hours. Approximately how many minutes did she spend with this client?
   A) 3.5 minutes
   B) 5.8 minutes
   C) 21 minutes
   D) 35 minutes

25) A flower store charges $24 for a small arrangement of flowers. A customer will get a $5 discount if he or she provides his or her own vase for the small arrangement. This month, there were 12 customers who ordered small arrangements and provided their own vases. How much money in total did the flower store make on arrangements sold to these 12 customers?
   A) $228
   B) $282
   C) $288
   D) $348

26) A bricklayer works for a construction company. He laid bricks for 7 hours per day for 4 days on one job. The customer was billed $45 per hour for his work, and the bricklayer was paid $25 per hour. After the bricklayer's wages have been paid, how much money did the company make on this job?
   A) $175
   B) $180
   C) $315
   D) $560

27) A pharmacist in a local drug store filled 250 prescriptions in 40 hours. Assuming that each prescription takes the same amount of time, how many minutes should it take the pharmacist to fill a single prescription?
   A) 0.16 minutes
   B) 1.6 minutes
   C) 3.75 minutes
   D) 9.6 minutes

28) A truck driver delivered 120 orders this week. She delivered 105 of the orders on time. What percentage of the driver's orders were delivered on time?
   A) 0.875%
   B) 8.75%
   C) 87.5%
   D) 0.125%

29) A scientist is measuring cell growth or attrition. Each day a measurement is taken. Cell growth is represented as a positive figure, while cell attrition is represented as a negative figure. On Monday cell growth was 27, and for all days Tuesday through Friday, cell attrition was 13 per day. What number represents total cell growth or attrition for these five days?
   A) 25
   B) −25
   C) 40
   D) −40

30) A vegetable farmer works until noon each day. The chart below shows the amounts of cucumbers per hour that she picked one morning:

   7:00 to 8:00   23 cucumbers
   8:00 to 9:00   25 cucumbers
   9:00 to 10:00   26 cucumbers
   10:00 to 11:00   24 cucumbers
   11:00 to 12:00   22 cucumbers

   On average, how many cucumbers did the farmer pick per hour?
   A) 23
   B) 24
   C) 25
   D) 26

31) A company makes concrete for construction jobs. When making one particular kind of concrete, you have to add 2 parts sand for every 3 parts of cement powder. You are currently making a batch of this concrete that has 66 parts of cement. How many parts sand should you add to this batch?
   A) 2
   B) 3
   C) 22
   D) 44

32) It is company policy that the ratio of employees to supervisors should be 50:1. So, for every 50 employees in a company, there should be 1 supervisor. If there are 255 employees in total, how many supervisors are there?
   A) 1
   B) 2
   C) 3
   D) 5

33) A report shows that 2 out of every 20 employees of a particular company are interested in applying for a promotion. If the company has 480 employees in total, how many employees are interested in applying for a promotion?
   A) 20
   B) 24
   C) 42
   D) 48

34) A mechanic spent from 8:10 to 8:22 changing three wheel covers on a car. At this rate, how many wheel covers could he change per hour?
   A) 3
   B) 5
   C) 10
   D) 15

35) A fencing company put up $15^2/_8$ yards of fence for one customer and $13^5/_8$ yards of fence for another customer. How many yards of fence did the company put up for both customers in total?
   A) $28^3/_8$
   B) $28^5/_8$
   C) $28^7/_8$
   D) $28^{10}/_{16}$

36) It is your job to fill gourmet food boxes with various products. So far today, you have filled $2^3/_8$ boxes for one order and $4^1/_8$ boxes for another order. How many total boxes have you filled so far today?
   A) $6^1/_2$
   B) $6^1/_4$
   C) $6^3/_4$
   D) $6^3/_{16}$

37) A customer has just placed an order for to have an awning made for his front window. According to the measurements, you will need $5^{3}/_{16}$ yards of canvas to make the awning. However, the customer calls later to say that his initial measurement was incorrect, and you now need only $4^{1}/_{16}$ yards of canvas to make the awning. Which fraction below represents the amount by which the amount of canvas has been reduced?
A) $1^{1}/_{8}$
B) $1^{1}/_{16}$
C) $1^{1}/_{32}$
D) $1^{3}/_{16}$

38) Certain additives need to be placed in a bottle to make a product. The company measures each additive in decimal units, with 1 unit representing the filled bottle. The bottle contains 0.25 units of additive A, 0.50 units of additive B, and 0.10 units of additive C. Which of the following represents, in terms of units, how full the bottle currently is?
A) 08.5
B) 0.85
C) 0.90
D) 0.95

39) Add: 102.5 + 1.38

40) Subtract: 94.7 − 13.2

HESI Math Practice Test 2 – Solutions and Explanations:

1) The correct answer is 15.

Substitute –2 for x to solve.

$2x^2 - x + 5 =$

$[2 \times (-2^2)] - (-2) + 5 =$

$[2 \times (4)] - (-2) + 5 =$

$(2 \times 4) + 2 + 5 =$

$8 + 2 + 5 = 15$

2) The correct answer is 4.

Isolate x to solve. You do this by doing the same operation on each side of the equation.

$-6x + 5 = -19$

Subtract 5 from each side to get rid of the integer 5 on the left side.

$-6x + 5 - 5 = -19 - 5$

Then simplify.

$-6x = -24$

Then divide each side by –6 to isolate x.

$-6x \div -6 = -24 \div -6$

$x = -24 \div -6$

$x = 4$

3) The correct answer is 5,556.48 grams.

The infant weighs 12 pounds 4 ounces, and we need to convert to grams.

Convert the pounds first.

1 pound = 453.59 grams

12 pounds × 453.59 = 5443.08 grams

Then convert the ounces.

1 ounce = 28.35 grams

4 ounces × 28.35 = 113.40 grams

Then add the two above results together to get the total grams.

5443.08 + 113.40 = 5,556.48 grams.

4) The correct answer is 95°F.

The temperature is is 35° Celsius

Use this formula to convert from Celsius to Fahrenheit: °F = 1.8(°C) + 32

Substitute 35° for (°C) in the formula to solve.

°F = 1.8(35°) + 32

°F = (1.8 × 35°) + 32

°F = 63 + 32

°F = 95

5) The correct answer is 8 hours.

She has worked from 1800 to 0200.

Convert to regular time first.

1800 to 0200 = (18 − 12) to 200 = 6:00 PM to 2:00 AM

If you still have difficulty solving after converting to regular time, then think about the how much time has passed before midnight, and how much time has passed after midnight.

From 6:00 PM to midnight, 6 hours have passed.

From midnight to 2:00 AM, 2 hours have passed.

Then add these two results together to get the total: 6 hours + 2 hours = 8 hours

6) The correct answer is 33.8.

You should memorize all of the conversions for your exam.

From the conversion chart in practice test 1, we know that 1 liter = 33.8 ounces.

7) The correct answer is 1,000 milliliters.

From the conversion chart in practice test 1, we know that 1 liter = 1,000 milliliters.

8) The correct answer is 100 centimeters.

Check the conversion chart in practice test 1 if you have had problems with the above questions. It states that 1 meter = 100 centimeters.

9) The correct answer is 128 ounces.

We are dealing with 4 quarts, and we want to convert the amount to ounces.

Convert the quarts to pints first.

1 quart = 2 pints

4 quarts × 2 = 8 pints

Then convert the pints to ounces.

1 pint = 16 ounces

8 pints × 16 = 128 ounces

10) The correct answer is 20.882 inches.

The newborn measures 53 cm in length.

1 cm = 0.394 inch

53 × 0.394 = 20.882 inches

11) The correct answer is D.

The sum of all contributions must be equal to 100%, simplified to 1. Let's say that the variable U represents the unfunded portion of the project.

So the equation that represents this problem is $A + B + U = 1$

Substitute with the fractions that have been provided.

$$\frac{1}{2} + \frac{1}{8} + U = 1$$

For problems with fractions, you often have to find the lowest common denominator.

Finding the lowest common denominator means that you have to make all of the numbers on the bottoms of the fractions the same.

Remember that you need to find the common factors of the denominators in order to find the LCD.

We know that 2 and 4 are factors of 8.

So, the LCD for this question is 8 since the denominator of the first fraction is 2 and because 2 × 4 = 8.

So, we put the fractions into the LCD as follows:

$$\frac{1}{2} + \frac{1}{8} + U = 1$$

Change $^1/_2$ to eighths with the common factor of 4.

$$\left(\frac{1}{2} \times \frac{4}{4}\right) + \frac{1}{8} + U = 1$$

$$\frac{1 \times 4}{2 \times 4} + \frac{1}{8} + U = 1$$

We are adding fractions that have a common denominator, so add the numerators.

$$\frac{4}{8} + \frac{1}{8} + U = 1$$

$$\frac{5}{8} + U = 1$$

Get rid of the fraction by subtracting it from both sides of the equation.

$$\frac{5}{8} - \frac{5}{8} + U = 1 - \frac{5}{8}$$

$$U = 1 - \frac{5}{8}$$

1 is equal to $^8/_8$, so put that in the equation to solve.

$$U = \frac{8}{8} - \frac{5}{8}$$

$$U = \frac{3}{8}$$

12) The correct answer is D.

For practical problems like this, you must first determine the percentage and formula that you need in order to solve the problem.

Then, you must do long multiplication to determine how many games the team won.

Be careful. The question tells you the percentage of games the team lost, not won.

So, first of all, we have to calculate the percentage of games won.

If the team lost 20 percent of the games, we know that the team won the remaining 80 percent.

Now do the long multiplication.

```
   50  games in total
× .80  percentage of games won (in decimal form)
 40.0  total games won
```

13) The correct answer is B.

First you need to find the total points that Carmen earned. You do this by taking Carmen's erroneous average times 4.

$4 \times 90 = 360$

Then you need to divide the total points earned by the correct number of tests in order to get the correct average.

$360 \div 5 = 72$

14) The correct answer is D.

You must first determine the percentage of questions that Beth answered correctly.

We know that she got 10% of the answers wrong, so therefore the remaining 90% were correct.

Now we multiply the total number of questions by the percentage of correct answers.

60 × 90% = 54

15) The correct answer is B.

Take the number of questions missed and add the extra credit points.

−36 + 25 = −11

Since the question is asking how much the score was lowered, you need to give the amount as a positive number.

16) The correct answer is D.

Convert the fractions in the mixed numbers to decimals.

$3/4 = 3 ÷ 4 = 0.75$

$1/5 = 1 ÷ 5 = 0.20$

Then represent the mixed numbers as decimal numbers

Person 1: $14^3/_4$ = 14.75

Person 2: $20^1/_5$ = 20.20

Person 3: 36.35

Then add all three amounts together to find the total.

14.75 + 20.20 + 36.35 = 71.30

17) The correct answer is D.

The sum of the work from all four people must be equal to 100%, simplified to 1. In other words, they make up the total hours by working together.

A + B + C + D = 1

$1/6 + 1/3 + 1/6 + D = 1$

Now find the lowest common denominator of the fractions.

3 × 2 = 6, so the lowest common denominator is 6.

The fractions for Person A and Person C already have 6 in their denominators, so we only have to convert the fraction for Person B.

Convert the fraction as required.

$1/3 \times 2/2 = 2/6$

Now add the fractions together.

$1/6 + 2/6 + 1/6 + D = 1$

$4/6 + D = 1$

$4/6 - 4/6 + D = 1 - 4/6$

$D = 1 - 4/6$

$D = 2/6$

$D = 1/3$

18) The correct answer is B.

First divide the total price for the multi-purchase by the number of items.

In this case, $150 ÷ 5 = $30 for each of the five books.

Then, subtract this amount from the original price to get your answer.

$40 − $30 = $10

Alternatively, you can use the method explained below.

Calculate the total price for the five books without the discount.

5 × $40 = $200

Then subtract the discounted price of $150 from the total.

$200 - $150 = $50

Then divide the total savings by the number of books to determine the savings on each book.

$50 total savings ÷ 5 books = $10 savings per book

19) The correct answer is D.

First of all, you have to calculate the total amount of points earned by the entire class.

Multiply the female average by the amount of female students.

Total points for female students: 87 × 55 = 4785

Then multiply the male average by the amount of male students.

Total points for male students: 80 × 45 = 3600

Then add these two amounts together to find out the total points scored by the entire class.

Total points for entire class: 4785 + 3600 = 8385

When you have calculated the total amount of points for the entire class, you divide this by the total number of students in the class to get the class average.

8385 ÷ 100 = 83.85

20) The correct answer is D.

We know that Mary has already gotten 80% of the money.

However, the question is asking how much money she still needs.

So, 100% − 80% = 20% and 20% = 0.20

Now do the multiplication.

650 × 0.20 = 130

21) The correct answer is D.

To solve this type of problem, do the multiplication on the items in parentheses first.

$5x - 2(x + 3) = 0$

$5x - 2x - 6 = 0$

Then deal with the integers by putting them on one side of the equation.

$5x - 2x - 6 + 6 = 0 + 6$

$3x = 6$

Then solve for x.

$3x = 6$

$x = 6 \div 3$

$x = 2$

22) The correct answer is D.

To solve this problem, put in the values for x and y and multiply. Remember that two negatives together make a positive.

For example, $-(-5) = 5$

So, be careful when multiplying negative numbers.

$6x^2 - xy + y^2 =$

$(6 \times 5^2) - (5 \times -1) + (-1^2) =$

$(6 \times 5 \times 5) - (-5) + 1 =$

$(6 \times 25) + 5 + 1 =$

$150 + 5 + 1 = 156$

23) The correct answer is D.

The two people are working at different costs per hour, so each person needs to be assigned a variable.

A is for the number of hours for the first person, and B is for the number of hours for the second person.

The cost for each person is calculated by taking the number of hours that the person works by the hourly wage for that person.

So, the equation for wages for the first person is $(7.25 \times A)$

The equation for the wages for the second person is $(10.50 \times B)$

The total cost of the wages for this job is the sum of the wages of these two people.

$(7.25 \times A) + (10.50 \times B) =$

(7.25A + 10.50B)

24) The correct answer is B.

The two tests are being given different percentages, so each test needs to have its own variable.

A for test A and B for test B.

Since A counts for 35% of the final grade, we set 35% to a decimal and put the decimal in front of the variable so that the variable will have the correct weight.

So, the value of test A is 0.35A

Test B counts for 65%, so the value of test B is 0.65B

The final grade is the sum of the values for the two tests.

So, we add the above products together to get our equation.

0.35A + 0.65B

25) The correct answer is C.

STEP 1: You can simplify the first fraction because both the numerator and denominator are divisible by 3: $3/9 \div 3/3 = 1/3$

STEP 2: Then divide the denominator of the second fraction ($x/21$) by the denominator of the simplified fraction ($1/3$) from above: 21 ÷ 3 = 7

STEP 3: Now, multiply the number from step 2 by the numerator of the fraction we calculated in step 1 in order to get your result: 1 × 7 = 7

26) The correct answer is 83.25

33.3 × 2.5 = ?

```
  33.3
× 2.5
─────
  1665
  6660
─────
  8325
```

There is one decimal place in 33.3 and one decimal place in 2.5, so our result must have two decimal places in total: 83.25

27) The correct answer is D.

Add the feet above ground to the feet below ground to get the total distance:

525 + 95 = 620 feet

28) The correct answer is C.

STEP 1: Add the items together to get the total amount of items available: 13 + 22 + 25 = 60

STEP 2: Divide the amount of items available by the number of people: 60 ÷ 12 = 5

29) The correct answer is B.

STEP 1: Determine the value of the discount by multiplying the normal price by the percentage discount: $90 × 15% = $13.50 discount.

STEP 2: Subtract the value of the discount from the normal price to get the new price:

$90 − $13.50 = $76.50

30) The correct answer is C.

STEP 1: You can express the fractions as decimals for the sake of simplicity.

10½ = 10.50; 7¾ = 7.75

STEP 2: Then subtract to find the increase: 10.50 − 7.75 = 2.75

STEP 3: Then convert back to a mixed number: 2.75 = 2¾

31) The correct answer is A.

After her raise, she earns $184 per week. She continues to work 23 hours per week.

STEP 1: Determine the new hourly rate: $184 ÷ 23 hours = $8 per hour

STEP 2: Determine the change in the hourly rate: $8 − $7.50 = 50 cents per hour

32) The correct answer is A.

STEP 1: Determine the distance traveled. If he is traveling 70 miles an hour, he will have traveled 70 miles after one hour has passed.

STEP 2: Determine the distance from the towns listed on the sign, considering that he has traveled for one hour.

Washington: 140 – 70 = 70 miles from Washington

Yorkville: 105 – 70 = 35 miles from Yorkville

Zorster: 210 – 70 = 140 miles from Zorster

STEP 3: Compare the above figures to your answer choices to get your result. After an hour, he is 70 miles from Washington, so A is correct.

33) The correct answer is D.

STEP 1: Subtract the excess from the total: 300 – 114 = 186

STEP 2: Allocate the difference into its respective parts. We are dividing the day into two parts: morning and afternoon. There were 186 cars in total without the excess, so divide this into two parts: 186 ÷ 2 = 93.

STEP 3: Determine the amount for the larger part. There were 114 more cars in the morning, so add this back in: 93 + 114 = 207 cars in the morning

34) The correct answer is B.

STEP 1: Think about the value of the four pairs of socks she is getting in the exchange. These socks cost 50 cents more each than the pairs she has already bought. So, we can express the difference in value of those four pairs of socks as: 4 × ($3 - $2.50)

STEP 2: Take into account the value of the extra pair of socks. She paid $2.50 for a fifth pair of socks, but she is only getting four pairs back on the exchange, so she is owed money back for that part of the purchase.

Therefore, we can calculate the refund owing as $2.50 – 4($3 – $2.50)

35) The correct answer is A.

The line in any fraction can be treated as the division symbol. Accordingly, we can divide by the denominator, which is 100 in this case.

$$\frac{35 \times 90}{100} = (35 \times 90) \div 100$$

36) The correct answer is C.

Each journey is 108 minutes (1 hour and 48 minutes) in duration.

So, we need to add 108 minutes to the departure time of 11:52 to get the arrival time of 1:40.

37) The correct answer is D.

A 12-pound container of item B costs $48.

Therefore, it costs $4 per pound ($48 ÷ 12 pounds = $4 per pound).

Item C costs 20% more per pound than item B.

In other words, Item C costs 80 cents more ($4 × 20% = 0.80).

So, the cost per pound of item C is $4.80.

38) The correct answer is B.

The cost of the photography course is $20 per week plus a $5 fee per week for review of photographs and administration. So, the course costs $25 per week. To get the total cost we need to multiply by the number of weeks, which is represented by variable W. Therefore, the total cost of the course and fees for W weeks is $25 × W = $25W.

39) The correct answer is 26.478

Add zeroes as placeholders and line up the decimal points.

7 + 13.45 + 6.028 =

```
 1
  7.000
 13.450
  6.028
 26.478
```

40) The correct answer is 26.45

Like when we add decimals, we need to add zeroes as placeholders and line up the decimal points. Cancel out as shown below.

32.7 − 6.25 =

$$\begin{array}{r} {\scriptstyle 2\,1\,\,6\,1} \\ \cancel{32.7}0 \\ \underline{6.25} \\ 26.45 \end{array}$$

HESI Math Practice Test 3 – Solutions and Explanations:

1) The correct answer is 28.

Substitute −3 for x and perform the operations to solve.

$3x^2 + 2x + 7$ if $x = -3$

$3(-3^2) + (2 \times -3) + 7 =$

$[3 \times (-3^2)] + (2 \times -3) + 7 =$

$[3 \times (9)] + (2 \times -3) + 7 =$

$(3 \times 9) + (2 \times -3) + 7 =$

$27 + (2 \times -3) + 7 =$

$27 + (-6) + 7 =$

$27 - 6 + 7 = 28$

2) The correct answer is −9.

Subtract 5 from each side of the equation first.

$3x + 5 = -22$

$3x + 5 - 5 = -22 - 5$

$3x = -22 - 5$

$3x = -27$

Divide each side by 3 to isolate x and solve.

$3x = -27$

$3x \div 3 = -27 \div 3$

$x = -27 \div 3$

$x = -9$

3) The correct answer is 165.1 centimeters.

The patient's height is 65 inches.

1 inch = 2.54 cm

65 × 2.54 = 165.1 cm

4) The correct answer is 37.52 °C.

The temperature is 99° Fahrenheit. Put the degrees into the equation to solve.

°C = 0.56(°F − 32)

°C = 0.56(99° − 32)

°C = 0.56(67)

°C = 0.56 × 67 =

°C = 37.52

5) The correct answer is D.

The nurse's usual shift is from 0000 to 0800.

0000 is midnight and 0800 is 8 AM, so answer D is correct.

6) The correct answer is 2.2 pounds.

The measurements chart in practice test 1 states that 1 kilogram = 2.2 pounds.

7) The correct answer is 10 millimeters.

The measurements chart in practice test 1 states that 1 centimeter = 10 millimeters.

8) The correct answer is 100.

"Conversion factor" means the number you need to multiply by to make the conversion.

1 meter = 100 centimeters, so the conversion factor to convert meters to centimeters is 100.

9) The correct answer is 960 milliliters.

Convert to ounces first.

1 pint = 16 ounces

2 pints × 16 = 32 ounces

Then convert ounces to milliliters.

1 ounce = 30 milliliters

32 × 30 = 960 milliliters

10) The correct answer is 12.538 kilograms.

The equipment weighs 12,538 grams.

1 gram = 0.001 kilograms

12,538 × 0.001 = 12.538 kilograms

11) The correct answer is D.

Because two negatives make a positive, we know that − (−6) = 6. So, we can substitute this into the equation in order to solve it: − (−6) + 2 = 6 + 2 = 8

12) The correct answer is C.

Multiply the numerators: 1 × 2 = 2. Then multiply the denominators: 5 × 3 = 15. These numbers form the new fraction: $2/15$

13) The correct answer is B.

Remember to invert the second fraction by putting the denominator on the top and the numerator on the bottom. So the second fraction $\frac{2}{3}$ becomes $\frac{3}{2}$ when inverted. Use the inverted fraction to solve the problem: $\frac{4}{7} \div \frac{2}{3} = \frac{4}{7} \times \frac{3}{2} = \frac{4 \times 3}{7 \times 2} = \frac{12}{14}$

14) The correct answer is A.

STEP 1: To find the LCD, you have to look at the factors for each denominator. Factors are the numbers that equal a product when they are multiplied by each other.

The factors of 8 are: 1 × **8** = 8; **2** × 4 = 8

The factors of 16 are: 1 × 16 = 16; **2** × **8** = 16; 4 × 4 = 16.

STEP 2: Determine which factors are common to both denominators by comparing the lists of factors. In this problem, the factors of 2 and 8 are common to the denominators of both fractions. (The numbers in bold above are the common factors.)

STEP 3: Multiply the common factors to get the lowest common denominator. The numbers that are in bold above are then used to calculate the lowest common denominator: 2 × 8 = 16.

STEP 4: Convert the denominator of each fraction to the LCD. You convert the fraction by referring to the factors from step 3. Multiply the numerator and the denominator by the same factor. We convert the first fraction as follows: $\frac{1}{8} \times \frac{2}{2} = \frac{2}{16}$. We do not need to convert the second fraction because it already has the LCD.

STEP 5: When both fractions have the same denominator, you can perform the operation to solve the problem: $\frac{2}{16} + \frac{3}{16} = \frac{5}{16}$

15) The correct answer is D.

STEP 1: Look at the factors of the numerator and denominator.

The factors of 12 are: 1 × 12 = 12; **2** × 6 = 12; 3 × 4 = 12.

The factors of 14 are: 1 × 14 = 14; **2** × 7 = 14. So, we can see that the numerator and denominator have the common factor of 2.

STEP 2: Simplify the fraction by dividing the numerator and denominator by the common factor. Simplify the numerator: 12 ÷ 2 = 6. Then simplify the denominator: 14 ÷ 2 = 7.

STEP 3: Use the results from step 2 to form the new fraction. The numerator from step 2 is 6. The denominator is 7. So, the new fraction is $\frac{6}{7}$.

16) The correct answer is C.

STEP 1: Convert the first mixed number to an integer plus a fraction.

$4\frac{1}{8} = 4 + \frac{1}{8}$

STEP 2: Then multiply the integer by a fraction whose numerator and denominator are the same as the denominator of the existing fraction:

$4 + \frac{1}{8} = \left(4 \times \frac{8}{8}\right) + \frac{1}{8} = \frac{4 \times 8}{8} + \frac{1}{8} = \frac{32}{8} + \frac{1}{8}$

STEP 3: Add the two fractions to get your new fraction: $\frac{32}{8} + \frac{1}{8} = \frac{33}{8}$

Convert the second mixed number to a fraction, using the same steps that we have just completed for the first mixed number: $3\frac{5}{6} = 3 + \frac{5}{6} = \left(3 \times \frac{6}{6}\right) + \frac{5}{6} = \frac{18}{6} + \frac{5}{6} = \frac{23}{6}$

Now that you have converted both mixed numbers to fractions, find the lowest common denominator and subtract to solve.

$\frac{33}{8} - \frac{23}{6} = \left(\frac{33}{8} \times \frac{3}{3}\right) - \left(\frac{23}{6} \times \frac{4}{4}\right) = \frac{(33 \times 3)}{(8 \times 3)} - \frac{(23 \times 4)}{(6 \times 4)} = \frac{99}{24} - \frac{92}{24} = \frac{99 - 92}{24} = \frac{7}{24}$

17) The correct answer is A.

Do the multiplication and division from left to right. So, take the number to the left of the multiplication or division symbol and multiply or divide that number by the number on the right of the symbol.

We need to multiply –5 by 4 and then divide 6 by 3. You can see the order of operations more clearly if you put in parentheses to group the numbers together.

–5 × 4 – 6 ÷ 3 = (–5 × 4) – (6 ÷ 3) = –20 – 2 = –22

18) The correct answer is C.

Determine the dollar amount of the reduction or discount:

$60 original price – $45 sale price = $15 discount

Then divide the discount by the original price to get the percentage of the discount:

$15 ÷ $60 = 0.25 = 25%

19) The correct answer is C.

The price of socks is $2 per pair and the price of shoes is $25 per pair, and Anna paid $85 in total. We know that she bought 3 pairs of shoes.

Remember to assign a different variable to each item.

Then make your equation by multiplying each variable by its price.

So, let's say that the number of pairs of socks is S and the number of pairs of shoes is H.

Your equation is:

$(S \times \$2) + (H \times \$25) = \$85$

We know that the number of pairs of shoes is 3, so put that in the equation and solve it.

$(S \times \$2) + (H \times \$25) = \$85$

$(S \times \$2) + (3 \times \$25) = \$85$

$(S \times \$2) + \$75 = \$85$

$(S \times \$2) + 75 - 75 = \$85 - \$75$

$(S \times \$2) = \$10$

$\$2S = \$10$

$\$2S \div 2 = \$10 \div 2$

$S = 5$

So, she bought 5 pairs of socks.

20) The correct answer is B.

Remember to assign variables to the items and then multiply each variable by its price.

The number of hot dogs is D and the number of hamburgers is H.

So, your equation is: $(D \times \$2.50) + (H \times \$4) = \$22$

The number of hamburgers is 3, so put that in the equation and solve it.

$(D \times \$2.50) + (H \times \$4) = \$22$

($D \times \$2.50$) + ($3 \times \$4$) = $22

($D \times \$2.50$) + 12 = $22

($D \times \$2.50$) + 12 − 12 = $22 − 12

($D \times \$2.50$) = $10

$2.50D = $10

$2.50D ÷ $2.50 = $10 ÷ $2.50

$D = 4$

21) The correct answer is C.

Work backwards based on the facts given. There are 18 students left at the end after one-fourth of them left for the principal's office. So, set up an equation for this, with T as the total number of students:

$18 + \frac{1}{4}T = T$

$18 + \frac{1}{4}T - \frac{1}{4}T = T - \frac{1}{4}T$

$18 = \frac{3}{4}T$

$18 \times 4 = \frac{3}{4}T \times 4$

$72 = 3T$

$72 \div 3 = 3T \div 3$

$24 = T$

So, before the group of pupils left to see the principal, there were 24 students in the class. We know that one-fifth of the students left at the beginning to go to singing lessons, so we need to set up an equation for this:

$24 + \frac{1}{5}T = T$

$24 + \frac{1}{5}T - \frac{1}{5}T = T - \frac{1}{5}T$

$24 = \frac{4}{5}T$

$24 \times 5 = {}^4/_5 T \times 5$

$120 = 4T$

$120 \div 4 = 4T \div 4$

$30 = T$

22) The correct answer is B.

At the beginning of January, there are 300 students, but 5% of the students leave during the month, so we have 95% left at the end of the month: 300 × 95% = 285.

Then 15 students join on the last day of the month, so we add that back in to get to the total at the end of January: 285 + 15 = 300. If this pattern continues, there will always be 300 students in the academy at the end of any month.

23) The correct answer is D.

Calculate the discount: $120 × 12.5% = $15 discount. Then subtract the discount from the original price to determine the sales price: $120 – $15 = $105

24) The correct answer is C.

Yesterday the train traveled $117^3/_4$ miles, and today it traveled $102^1/_6$ miles. To find the difference, we subtract these two amounts. Because the fraction on the first mixed number is greater than the fraction on the second mixed number, we can subtract the whole numbers and the fractions separately: $117^3/_4$ miles – $102^1/_6$ miles = ?

STEP 1: Subtract the whole numbers: 117 – 102 = 15 miles.

STEP 2: Perform the operation on the fractions by finding the lowest common denominator.

$^3/_4$ miles – $^1/_6$ miles = ? In order to find the LCD, we would normally need to find the common factors first. Our denominators in this problem are 4 and 6.

The factors of 4 are: 1 × 4 = 4; 2 × 2 = 4. The factors of 6 are: 1 × 6 = 6; 2 × 3 = 6. We do not have two factors in common, so we know that we need to find a new denominator which is greater than 6. In this problem, the LCD is 12 since 3 × 4 = 12 and 2 × 6 = 12. So, we express the fractions $^3/_4$ miles + $^1/_6$ miles in their LCD form: $^3/_4 \times ^3/_3 = ^9/_{12}$ and $^1/_6 \times ^2/_2 = ^2/_{12}$. Then subtract these two fractions: $^9/_{12} - ^2/_{12} = ^7/_{12}$

STEP 3: Combine the results from the two previous steps to solve the problem:

$117^3/_4$ miles − $102^1/_6$ miles = $15^7/_{12}$ miles

25) The correct answer is D.

Sam is driving at 70 miles per hour, and at 10:30 am he is 140 miles from Farnam.

STEP 1: We need to find out how far he will be from Farnam at 11:00 am, so we need to work out how far he will travel in 30 minutes.

STEP 2: If Sam is traveling at 70 miles an hour, then he travels 35 minutes in half an hour:

70 miles in one hour × $^1/_2$ hour = 35 miles

STEP 3: If he was 140 miles from Farnam at 10:30 am, he will be 105 miles from Farnam at 11:00 am: 140 − 35 = 105 miles

26) The correct answer is C.

The twelve students who failed the test represent one-third of the class. Since one-third of the students have failed, we can think of the class as being divided into three groups:

Group 1: The 12 students who failed; Group 2: 12 students who would have passed; Group 3: 12 more students who would have passed. So, the class consists of 36 students in total. In other words, we need to multiply by three to find the total number of students: 12 × 3 = 36

27) The correct answer is B.

The problem tells us that sales this week were $600 and sales last week were $525.

STEP 1: First, we need to find the difference in sales between the two weeks:

$600 - $525 = $75 more in sales this week

STEP 2: Since each book is sold for $5, we divide this figure into the total in order to find out how many books were sold: $75 more sales ÷ $5 per book = 15 more books sold this week

28) The correct answer is D.

A percentage can always be expressed as a number with two decimal places. For example, 15% = 0.15 and 20% = 0.20. In our problem, 16% = 0.16. So D is correct.

29) The correct answer is B.

STEP 1: First of all, you need to calculate the amount of the discount.

$18 original price × 40% = $18 × 0.40 = $7.20 discount

STEP 2: Then deduct the amount of the discount from the original price to calculate the sales price of the item: $18 original price – $7.20 discount = $10.80 sales price

30) The correct answer is A.

Find the average of your two exams: (85 + 91) ÷ 2 = 176 ÷ 2 = 88

Then deduct 2 points from this average for every day you missed class. You were absent 3 times, and 2 points are deducted per absence, so 6 points are to be deducted in total.

88 – 6 = 82

31) The correct answer is C.

STEP 1: Calculate the amount of the tax increase: $480 × 7.5% = ?

$480 original tax amount × 0.075 = $36 proposed increase in tax

STEP 2: Then add the increase to the original amount to get the amount of the tax after the proposed increase: $480 original tax + $36 increase in tax = $516 tax after increase

32) The correct answer is B.

If there are 12 children and each one is supposed to receive 4 items, we can do the calculation as follows: 12 children × 4 items per child = 48 items required in total. Now subtract the total from the amount she already has in order to determine how many more she needs:

48 items required in total – 40 items available = 8 items still needed

33) The correct answer is C.

First of all, you have to find out how many students were absent on Tuesday.

To find the number of absent students, you have to multiply the total number of students in the class by the percentage of the absence for Tuesday.

20 students in total × 5% = 1 student absent on Tuesday

Now calculate the absences for Wednesday in the same way:

20 students in total × 20% = 4 students absent on Wednesday

The problem is asking you how many more students were absent on Wednesday than Tuesday, so you need to subtract the two figures that you have just calculated.

4 students absent on Wednesday – 1 student absent on Tuesday = 3 students

So, 3 more students were absent on Wednesday.

34) The correct answer is B.

Substitute 5 for the value of x to solve.

$x^2 + xy - y = 41$

$5^2 + 5y - y = 41$

$25 + 5y - y = 41$

$25 - 25 + 5y - y = 41 - 25$

$5y - y = 16$

$4y = 16$

$4y \div 4 = 16 \div 4$

$y = 4$

35) The correct answer is B.

Remember to do multiplication on the items in parentheses first.

$4x - 3(x + 2) = -3$

$4x - 3x - 6 = -3$

Then deal with the integers.

$4x - 3x - 6 + 6 = -3 + 6$

$4x - 3x = 3$

Then solve for x.

$4x - 3x = 3$

$x = 3$

36) The correct answer is 1.066

When you see two numbers in parentheses placed together like this, you need to multiply.

Put in zeroes as placeholders and multiply as shown.

$(8.2)(0.13) =$

```
    8.2
×  0.13
    246
    820
  1.066
```

We have to move the decimal point 3 places from the right in our answer because 8.2 has 1 decimal place and 0.13 has two decimal places, so there are 3 decimal places in total.

37) The correct answer is 1062.5

$425 × 2.5 =$

```
   425
×  2.5
  2125
  8500
 10625
```

There is one decimal place in 2.5, so we need to put one decimal place in our answer: 1062.5

38) The correct answer is 11.873

Line up the decimals and cancel out where needed as shown below.

12.013 − 0.14 =

```
   1 9 1
 12.0̶13
− 0.140
 11.873
```

39) The correct answer is 7.7

14.9 − 7.2 =

```
  14.9
− 7.2
  7.7
```

40) The correct answer is 43.215

Line up the decimals, and add placeholders where needed. Don't forget to carry the 1.

35.2 + 8.015 =

```
 1
 35.200
+ 8.015
 43.215
```

HESI Math Practice Test 4 – Solutions and Explanations:

1) The correct answer is 15.

Substitute 8 for x to solve.

$x^2 - 5x - 9 =$

$8^2 - (5 \times 8) - 9 =$

$64 - 40 - 9 =$

15

2) The correct answer is 3.

$5x - 9 = 6$

Get rid of the integer on the left by adding 9 to each side of the equation.

$5x - 9 + 9 = 6 + 9$

$5x = 15$

Then divide each side by 5 to isolate x and solve.

$5x \div 5 = 15 \div 5$

$x = 3$

3) The correct answer is 700 milligrams.

1 gram = 1,000 milligrams

0.7 grams × 1000 = 700 milligrams

4) The correct answer is 120.2 °F.

The temperature is 49° Celsius.

Use the equation to convert to Fahrenheit: °F = 1.8(°C) + 32

°F = 1.8(°49) + 32

°F = 88.2 + 32

°F = 120.2°

5) The correct answer is 32 ounces.

1 cup = 8 ounces

4 cups × 8 = 32 ounces

6) The correct answer is 64 quarts.

1 gallon = 4 quarts

16 gallons × 4 = 64 quarts

7) The correct answer is 1,000 yards per day.

The patients need to walk 21,000 feet per week.

The formula states that: 1 yard = 3 feet

However, the equation is converting yards to feet, not feet to yards.

So, we need to divide by the conversion factor.

21,000 feet per week ÷ 3 = 7,000 yards per week

7,000 yards per week ÷ 7 days in a week = 1,000 yards per day

8) The correct answer is 437 pints and 8 ounces.

We are converting milliliters to pints and ounces, and we have 200,000 milliliters.

First, convert the milliliters to ounces.

1 milliliter = 0.035 ounce

200,000 × 0.035 = 7,000 ounces

Then convert the total ounces to pints and ounces.

We have 7,000 ounces.

The formula states that: 1 pint = 16 ounces

The formula is for converting pints to ounces, but we are converting ounces to pints.

Since we are working the formula backwards, we need to divide by the conversion factor.

7,000 ounces ÷ 16 = 437.5 pints

Finally, you have to convert the decimal to the number of ounces.

0.5 pints × 16 ounces = 8 ounces

So, the answer is 437 pints and 8 ounces.

9) The correct answer is 1,760 yards.

The formula states that: 1 mile = 1,760 yards

10) The correct answer is 500 kilometers.

You need to travel 500,000 meters.

The formula is: 1 meter = 0.001 kilometer

500,000 meters × 0.001 = 500 kilometers

11) The correct answer is B.

In our problem, if s% have been absent, then 100% − s% have not been absent. In other words, since a percentage is any given number out of 100%, the percentage of students who have not been absent is: (100% − s%). This equation is then multiplied by the total number of students (x) in order to determine the answer: (100% − s%) × x

12) The correct answer is B.

Line up the numbers by the comma, and remember to carry the 1's.

```
  1 1 1
  1,594
+23,786
 25,380
```

13) The correct answer is A.

Multiply 25 times $15 to get the answer: 25 × $15 = $375

14) The correct answer is A.

Line the figures up in a column and add zeroes as placeholders as shown below:

0.3500
0.0350
0.0530
0.3035

If you still struggle with decimals, you can remove the decimal points and the zeroes before the other integers in order to see the answer more clearly.

0̶.̶3500
0̶.̶0̶350
0̶.̶0̶530
0̶.̶3035

When we have removed the zeroes in front of the other numbers, we can clearly see that the largest number is 0.35.

15) The correct answer is A.

The equation is: F = $500P + $3,700. We are told that the total funds are $40,000 so put that in the equation to solve the problem.

$40,000 = $500P + $3,700

$40,000 − $3,700 = $500P

$36,300 = $500P

$36,300 ÷ 500 = $500 ÷ 500P

$36,300 ÷ 500 = 72.6

Since a fraction of a project cannot be undertaken, the greatest number of complete projects is 72.

16) The correct answer is D.

To answer this type of question, you need these principles: (a) Positive numbers are greater than negative numbers; (b) When two fractions have the same numerator, the fraction with the smaller number in the denominator is the larger fraction. Accordingly, 1 is greater than $1/5$; $1/5$ is greater than $1/7$, and $1/7$ is greater than $-1/3$.

17) The correct answer is A.

The problem tells us that the morning flight had 52 passengers more than the evening flight, and there were 540 passengers in total on the two flights that day.

Step 1: First of all, we need to deduct the difference from the total: 540 − 52 = 488; In other words, there were 488 passengers on both flights combined, plus the 52 additional passengers on the morning flight.

Step 2: Now divide this result by 2 to allocate an amount of passengers to each flight:

488 ÷ 2 = 244 passengers on the evening flight

Had the question asked you for the amount of passengers on the morning flight, you would have had to add back the amount of additional passengers to find the total amount of passengers for the morning flight: 244 + 52 = 296 passengers on the morning flight

18) The correct answer is C.

Divide and then round up: 82 people in total ÷ 15 people served per container = 5.467 containers. We need to round up to 6 since we cannot purchase a fractional part of a container.

19) The correct answer is A.

You need to create an equation to set out the facts of this problem. Here we will say that the total number of students is variable S.

$15 = (S - ¼S) \times ½$

$15 = ¾S \times ½$

$15 = ³/_8 S$

$15 \times 8 = ³/_8 S \times 8$

$120 = 3S$

$S = 40$

20) The correct answer is C.

Remember that the order of operations is PEMDAS: Parentheses, Exponents, Multiplication, Division, Addition, and Subtraction. There are no operations with parentheses, exponents, or multiplication. So, do the division first: 9 ÷ 3 = 3. Then replace this in the equation:

82 + 9 ÷ 3 − 5 = 82 + 3 − 5 = 80

21) The correct answer is A.

This is another problem on the order of operations. There are no operations with parentheses or exponents, so do the multiplication first: 6 × 3 = 18. Then put this number in the equation:

52 + 6 × 3 − 48 = 52 + 18 − 48 = 22

22) The correct answer is C.

In order to convert a fraction to a decimal, you must divide.

```
      .25
16)4.00
    3.2
    0.80
    0.80
       0
```

23) The correct answer is D.

30 percent in decimal form equals to 0.30. The phrase "of what number" shows that we have to divide: $90 \div 0.30 = 300$. We can check this result as follows: $300 \times 0.30 = 90$

24) The correct answer is A.

Questions like this test your knowledge of mixed numbers. Mixed numbers are those that contain a whole number and a fraction. If the fraction on the first mixed number is greater than the fraction on the second mixed number, you can subtract the whole numbers and the fractions separately. Remember to use the lowest common denominator on the fractions. First, subtract whole numbers: $6 - 2 = 4$

Then subtract fractions.

$3/4 - 1/2 =$

$3/4 - 2/4 =$

$1/4$

Now put them together for the result.

$4^1/_4$

25) The correct answer is D.

Remember PEMDAS: Parentheses, Exponents, Multiplication, Division, Addition, and Subtraction. So, you must do the division and multiplication first, before adding or subtracting.

We know that $9 \times 6 = 54$ and $42 \div 6 = 7$ so perform the operations and simplify:

$(9 \times 6) + (42 \div 6) = 54 + 7 = 61$

26) The correct answer is B.

To find the total amount contributed, you need to multiply.

31 × 12 = 372

27) The correct answer is D.

When you are asked to divide fractions, remember that you need to invert the second fraction. Then you multiply this inverted fraction by the first fraction given in the problem. $^4/_3$ inverted is $^3/_4$. Then multiply the numerators and the denominators together to get the new fraction.

$$\frac{1}{8} \div \frac{4}{3} =$$

$$\frac{1}{8} \times \frac{3}{4} =$$

$$\frac{3}{32}$$

28) The correct answer is C.

Remember that to represent a fraction as a decimal, you need to divide. So, you will need to do long division to determine the answer.

```
      .10
50)5.00
    5.00
       0
```

29) The correct answer is D.

Be careful not to confuse remainders with decimals. The remainder is the whole number amount left over after you have used whole numbers to divide.

```
    66
9)600
   54
   60
   54
    6   This is the remainder.
```

30) The correct answer is A.

This question assesses your knowledge of mixed numbers. In this problem, the fraction on the second number is bigger than the fraction on the first number. So, we have to convert the mixed numbers to fractions first.

$$3\tfrac{1}{2} - 2\tfrac{3}{5} = \left[\left(3 \times \tfrac{2}{2}\right) + \tfrac{1}{2}\right] - \left[\left(2 \times \tfrac{5}{5}\right) + \tfrac{3}{5}\right] =$$

$$\left(\tfrac{6}{2} + \tfrac{1}{2}\right) - \left(\tfrac{10}{5} + \tfrac{3}{5}\right) =$$

$$\tfrac{7}{2} - \tfrac{13}{5}$$

Then find the lowest common denominator.

$$\tfrac{7}{2} - \tfrac{13}{5} = \left(\tfrac{7}{2} \times \tfrac{5}{5}\right) - \left(\tfrac{13}{5} \times \tfrac{2}{2}\right) =$$

$$\tfrac{35}{10} - \tfrac{26}{10} = \tfrac{9}{10}$$

31) The correct answer is B.

Your equation is: (A × $5) + (B × $8) = $60. They buy 4 of product A, so put that in the equation and solve it.

(A × $5) + (B × $8) = $60

(4 × $5) + (B × $8) = $60

$20 + (B × $8) = $60

(B × $8) = $40

B = 5

32) The correct answer is 3.912

Line up the decimal points and carry the one where needed.

3.75 + 0.162 =

1
3.750
+ 0.162
3.912

33) The correct answer is B.

STEP 1: Look to see what information is common to both the question and to the information provided. Here we have the information that he can run 3 miles in 25 minutes. The question is asking how long it will take him to run 12 miles, so the commonality is miles.

STEP 2: Next, calculate how many 3-mile increments there are in 12 miles: 12 ÷ 3 = 4

STEP 3: Then you need to determine the time required to travel the stated distance. Accordingly, we need to multiply the time for 3 miles by 4: 25 minutes × 4 = 100

So, 100 minutes are needed to run 12 miles.

STEP 4: Finally, simplify into hours and minutes based on the fact that there are 60 minutes in one hour: 100 minutes = 1 hour 40 minutes

34) The correct answer is A.

STEP 1: First of all, we need to find out how many pieces of candy there are in total:

43 + 28 + 31 = 102 total pieces of candy

STEP 2: We need to divide the total amount of candy by the number of students in order to find out how much candy each student will get:

102 total pieces of candy ÷ 34 students = 3 pieces of candy per student

35) The correct answer is A.

The problem tells us that $x = 3$ and $y = -3$. So, put in the values for x and y and multiply.

$2x^2 + 3xy - y^2 =$

$(2 \times 3^2) + (3 \times 3 \times -3) - (-3^2) =$

$(2 \times 3 \times 3) + (3 \times 3 \times -3) - (-3 \times -3) =$

$18 + (-27) - 9 = -18$

36) The correct answer is C.

Add the percentages together to solve: 25% + 50% = 75%

37) The correct answer is D.

Step 1 – Multiply the whole numbers: 5 × 1 = 5

Step 2 – Multiply the whole number with the fraction: 5 × $\frac{1}{4}$ = $\frac{5}{4}$

Step 3 – Convert the fraction from Step 2 to a mixed number: $\frac{5}{4}$ = $1\frac{1}{4}$

Step 4 – Combine these two results to get your new mixed number: 5 + $1\frac{1}{4}$ = $6\frac{1}{4}$

Step 5 – Convert to hours and minutes: $6\frac{1}{4}$ hours = 6 hours and 15 minutes

38) The correct answer is 13.94

```
    82
×  0.17
   574
   820
  1394
```

0.17 has two decimal places and 82 has no decimal places, so we need 2 total decimal places in our result: 13.94

39) The correct answer is 93.106

Line up the decimal places using zeroes as placeholders, and cancel out as needed.

101.5 – 8.394 =

```
   9 1 4 9 1
  1̶0̶1̶.5̶0̶0̶
 −    8.394
     93.106
```

40) The correct answer is 16.4

13.6 + 2.8

```
   13.6
 +  2.8
   16.4
```

HESI Math Practice Test 5 – Solutions and Explanations:

1) The correct answer is –3.

Add 9 to each side to get rid of the integer on the left.

$3x - 9 = -18$

$3x - 9 + 9 = -18 + 9$

$3x = -9$

Then divide each side by 3 to solve.

$3x \div 3 = -9 \div 3$

$x = -3$

2) The correct answer is 154.

Substitute 7 for x to solve.

$2x^2 + 8x =$

$[2(7)^2] + (8 \times 7) =$

$(2 \times 49) + 56 =$

$98 + 56 = 154$

3) The correct answer is 16 ounces.

The formula states that: 1 pound = 16 ounces

4) The correct answer is 24.64 °C.

The temperature is 76° Fahrenheit.

The formula to convert Fahrenheit to Celsius is: °C = 0.56(°F – 32)

°C = 0.56(°76 – 32)

°C = 0.56(44)

°C = 24.64

5) The correct answer is 6.3 kilograms.

We need to convert pounds to kilograms.

The formula is: 1 pound = 0.45 kilogram

14 pounds × 0.45 = 6.3 kilograms

6) The correct answer is 1,000 grams.

The formula states that: 1 kilogram = 1,000 grams

7) The correct answer is 25.35 ounces.

We have 0.75 liter, and we need to convert to ounces.

1 liter = 33.8 ounces

0.75 liter × 33.8 = 25.35 ounces

8) The correct answer is 3,500 pounds.

The car weighs 1.75 tons, and we need to convert to pounds.

1 ton = 2,000 pounds

1.75 ton × 2,000 = 3,500 pounds

9) The correct answer is 512 ounces.

1 gallon = 128 ounces

4 gallons × 128 = 512 ounces

10) The correct answer is 63,360 inches.

1 mile = 5,280 feet and 1 foot = 12 inches.

5,280 feet × 12 = 63,360 inches

11) The correct answer is C.

The problem is asking for the total for all three years, so we add the three figures together:

$25,135 + $32,787 + $47,004 = $104,926

12) The correct answer is D.

For questions that ask you to calculate the change given to a customer, you need to take the amount of money the customer gives and subtract the amount of the purchase from this:

$50.00 − $41.28 = $8.72

13) The correct answer is D.

Multiplication problems will often include the words "each" or "every." The problem states that the salesperson earns a $175 referral fee on *every* customer, so he earned the referral fee 8 times this month. We need to multiply the amount of the referral fee by the number of customers to solve: $175 × 8 = $1400

14) The correct answer is C.

Division problems will often include the word "per." The problem states that you work 30 hours *per* week. So, divide the total weekly amount by the number of hours to solve:

$535.50 ÷ 30 = $17.85

15) The correct answer is B.

When you have to add a negative number to a positive number, you are really subtracting. So, add the business profits and subtract the business losses: 953 + 1502 − 286 − 107 = 2062

16) The correct answer is A.

In this problem, we need to subtract the depth of Lake Bajo from the location below sea level of Lake Alto. The location below sea level of Lake Alto is a negative number, so we subtract as follows: −35 − 62 = −97. Remember to express your result as a negative number.

17) The correct answer is B.

In order to express a fraction as a decimal, treat the line in the fraction as the division symbol: $3/5$ = 3 ÷ 5 = 0.60. Be careful with the decimal placement in your final result.

18) The correct answer is C.

To express a decimal number as a percent, move the decimal point two places to the right and add the percent sign: 0.55 = 55.0%

19) The correct answer is D.

In order to express a fraction as a percentage, you need to divide and then express the result as a percentage.

Step 1 – Treat the line in the fraction as the division symbol: $5/14$ = 5 ÷ 14 = 0.357

Step 2 – To express the result from Step 1 as a percentage, we need to move the decimal point two places to the right and add the percent sign: 0.357 = 35.7%

20) The correct answer is D.

For your exam, you should be able to recognize the equivalent fractions for commonly-used decimal numbers. If you are unsure, perform division on the answer choices to check:

$3/4$ = 3 ÷ 4 = 0.75

21) The correct answer is A.

For your exam, you should be able to recognize the equivalent fractions for commonly-used percentages. If you are unsure, perform division on the answer choices to check:

$1/3$ = 1 ÷ 3 = 0.3333 = 33%

22) The correct answer is C.

Any given percentage is out of 100%, so we divide by 100 to express a percentage as a decimal. So, move the decimal point two places to the left and remove the percent sign:

45% = 45 ÷ 100 = 0.45

23) The correct answer is B.

Express both amounts as decimal numbers and multiply to solve:

$14^1/_4$ pounds × 36 cents per pound = 14.25 × 0.36 = $5.13

24) The correct answer is C.

There are 60 minutes in an hour, so multiply the minutes in the hour by the decimal number given in the problem to solve: 60 minutes × 0.35 hour = 60 × 0.35 = 21 minutes

25) The correct answer is A.

Step 1 – Subtract the discount from the original price: $24 – $5 = $19

Step 2 – Take the result from Step 1 and multiply by the number of units sold: $19 × 12 = $228

26) The correct answer is D.

Step 1 – Determine the total number of hours worked: 7 hours per × 4 days = 28 hours

Step 2 – Calculate the profit the company makes per hour: The customer was billed $45 per hour for the work, and the employee was paid $25 per hour: $45 – $25 = $20 profit per hour

Step 3 – Multiply the total number of hours by the profit per hour to solve:

28 hours × $20 profit per hour = 28 × 20 = $560.

27) The correct answer is D.

Step 1 – Calculate the total time in minutes: 40 hours × 60 minutes = 2400 minutes

Step 2 – Take the result from Step 1 and divide by the number of prescriptions to solve:

2400 minutes ÷ 250 prescriptions = 9.6 minutes each

28) The correct answer is C.

The orders that were delivered on time are part of the total orders. So, take the amount of orders that were delivered on time and divide by the amount of total orders: 105 ÷ 120 = 0.875 = 87.5%

29) The correct answer is B.

On Monday cell growth was 27, and for all of the days Tuesday through Friday, cell attrition was 13 per day.

Step 1 – Cell attrition is a negative number, so perform multiplication to get the total for the four days (Tuesday through Friday): –13 × 4 = –52

Step 2 – On Monday cell growth was 27, so add this to the result from Step 1 to solve:

−52 + 27 = −25

30) The correct answer is B.

To find the average, you need to find the total, and then divide the total by the number of hours.

Step 1 – Find the total: 23 + 25 + 26 + 24 + 22 = 120

Step 2 – Divide the result from Step 1 by the number of hours: 120 ÷ 5 = 24

31) The correct answer is D.

Step 1 – Take the 66 parts cement for the current batch and divide by the 3 parts stated in the original ratio: 22 ÷ 3 = 22

Step 2 – Multiply the result from Step 1 by the 2 parts sand stated in the original ratio to get your answer: 2 × 22 = 44

32) The correct answer is D.

The problem states that we are working with a ratio, so the employees and the supervisors form separate groups.

Step 1 – Add the two groups together: 50 + 1 = 51

Step 2 – Take the total amount of employees stated in the problem and divide this by the figure calculated in Step 1 to get the amount of supervisors: 255 ÷ 51 = 5

33) The correct answer is D.

The problem uses the phrase "2 out of every 20 employees" so we know that there are 2 employees who form a subset within each group of 20.

Step 1 – Take the total number of employees and divide this by 20: 480 ÷ 20 = 24

Step 2 – Take the result from Step 1 and multiply by the amount in the subset to solve:

24 × 2 = 48

34) The correct answer is D.

Step 1 – Calculate the amount of time spent on the initial job: 8:10 to 8:22 = 12 minutes

Step 2 – Calculate how many increments of 12 minutes there are in an hour:

60 minutes ÷ 12 minutes = 5

Step 3 – Multiply the figure from Step 2 by the number of wheels changed during each 12 minute session to solve: 5 × 3 = 15

35) The correct answer is C.

Step 1 – Add the whole numbers. The whole numbers are the numbers in front of the fractions:

15 + 13 = 28

Step 2 – Add the fractions. If you have two fractions that have the same denominator, you add the numerators and keep the common denominator: $2/8 + 5/8 = 7/8$

Step 3 – Combine the results from Step 1 and Step 2 to get your new mixed number to solve the problem: $28 + 7/8 = 28\,7/8$

36) The correct answer is A.

Step 1 – Add the whole numbers: 2 + 4 = 6

Step 2 – Add the fractions. If you have two fractions that have the same denominator, you add the numerators and keep the common denominator: $1/8 + 3/8 = 4/8$

Step 3 – Simplify the fraction from Step 2: $4/8 = 1/2$

Step 4 – Combine the results from Step 1 and Step 3 to get your new mixed number to solve the problem: $6 + 1/2 = 6\,1/2$

37) The correct answer is A.

Step 1 – Subtract the whole numbers: 5 – 4 = 1

Step 2 – Subtract the fractions. If you have two fractions that have the same denominator, you subtract the numerators and keep the common denominator: $3/16 - 1/16 = 2/16$

Step 3 – Simplify the fraction from Step 2: $2/16 = 1/8$

Step 4 – Combine the results from Step 1 and Step 3 to get your new mixed number to solve the problem: $1 + {}^1/_8 = 1{}^1/_8$

38) The correct answer is B.

Add the three figures together to solve: $0.25 + 0.50 + 0.10 = 0.85$. Remember to be sure to put the decimal point in the correct place when you work out the solution to problems like this one.

39) The correct answer is 103.88

$102.5 + 1.38 =$

```
  102.50
+   1.38
  ------
  103.88
```

40) The correct answer is 81.5

$94.7 - 13.2 =$

```
   94.7
 - 13.2
  -----
   81.5
```

www.ingramcontent.com/pod-product-compliance
Lightning Source LLC
Chambersburg PA
CBHW060426010526
44118CB00017B/2371